THE FORBES COLLECTION

TOY BOATS

A CENTURY OF TREASURES
FROM SAILBOATS TO SUBMARINES

by Richard Scholl
Introduction by Robert L. Forbes

COURAGE
BOOKS

AN IMPRINT OF RUNNING PRESS
PHILADELPHIA · LONDON

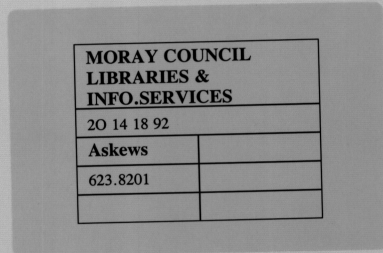
Library of Congress Control Number: 2004105752

ISBN 0-7624-1878-8

Cover and interior design by Frances J. Soo Ping Chow
Edited by Michael Washburn and Jennifer Leczkowski
Typography: Abadi, Adobe Caslon and Perpetua Titling

This book may be ordered by mail from the publisher.
But try your bookstore first!

Published by Courage Books, an imprint of
Running Press Book Publishers
125 South Twenty-second Street
Philadelphia, Pennsylvania 19103-4399

Visit us on the web!
www.runningpress.com

TABLE OF CONTENTS

Acknowledgments 4

Introduction by Robert L. Forbes 6

Chapter 1: The Birth and Growth of a Grand Collection 11

Chapter 2: Welcome to "Ships Ahoy!" in the Heart of the Forbes Galleries 21

Chapter 3: From the *Lusitania* to the *Missouri*,

      Toy Boats Reflect the Times 31

Chapter 4: The Great Toy Boat Companies Arose Together in Nuremberg 47

Chapter 5: What Makes These Boats So Rare and Valuable? 59

Chapter 6: Meet Some of the Brightest Stars in the Collection 67

An Interview With Robert L. Forbes 73

Bibliography 78

Battleship Picture Puzzle Cubes McLouglin Bros. 11" x 13¼"

ACKNOWLEDGMENTS

This book simply could not have been completed without the hospitality and aid of the staff at the Forbes Galleries in New York. The author wishes to thank Margaret Kelly Trombly, Vice President of the Forbes Collection, and her staff who made their files available for the research needed to complete this book. The author is also indebted to Gabrielle Schickler, Curator; Bonnie S. Kirschstein, Managing Director; and Allison Beth Sawczyn, Office Coordinator. The agent representing The Forbes Collection™, Joan G. Stanley of J.G. Stanley & Co., Inc., was invaluable as a liaison between the Forbes Galleries and both the publisher and the author. The author wishes to thank Robert Forbes for his superb introduction and insightful answers to questions posed in an interview that is presented in its entirety within these pages. We also wish to thank Robert Forbes, John Ehrenclou, and Paul Rider for their vivid photography of the toy boats housed in the Forbes Galleries. The publisher, Running Press, was represented by Michael Washburn and Jennifer Leczkowski, who provided essential editorship and coordination of the photos.

Note: The Forbes Galleries are located at 62 Fifth Avenue, New York City, and are open free to the public Tuesday through Saturdays, 10 A.M. to 4 P.M. Thursdays are for groups by appointment only.

Unpainted Tin Boat

INTRODUCTION

by Robert L. Forbes

Our infatuation with toy boats can be traced not just to my own childhood but back to my father's as well. As he put it, "Toy boats in the Forbes family were more prized than electric trains or other playthings. We were forever sailing them in nearby brooks and streams, and in summer on lakes or oceans." Despite the pleasure my siblings and I received from various boats given to us on birthdays or at Christmas, not a single one survived the rough waters of childhood to be part of the collection displayed at the Forbes Galleries and shown on these pages. And that is actually why toy boats are rare—why antique toy boats survived far less than other old toys: they were played with! Most toys, when

as he passed the antique toy counter, he saw an old friend—a boat similar to the ones he'd had as a child. He bought it and soon found he could, at last, get hold of the great toy boats he'd wanted those many years ago. He found that there was a whole network of antique toy collectors whose passions were trains, cars, and dolls. But where were the boats? He quickly recruited me to help him on his mission. A former bathtub admiral myself, I was eager to join the search. Word spread that there was a collector interested in boats. Soon owners and dealers were calling and sending photos of the one or two examples they had in their collections that showed what else a particular manufacturer made; they were happy to sell to us.

THE BOAT IS A COMPLETE TOY, ITS WORLD LIMITED ONLY

BY THE IMAGINATION OF ITS CAPTAIN

play was over, went back into their box or into a trunk for later use. But for toy boats, being played with often spelled disaster, because water (especially salt water) is metal's enemy by means of corrosive rust.

In the tub, recovering a sunken boat was easy, though the resulting rust eventually took its toll. But the most fun for a child was to play with it, by sailing it on lakes and at seashores where so often the clockwork mechanism wound down when the ship was out of reach. Sometimes a steam-powered boat even blew up! As with real ones, the more toy boats did their thing the less likely they were to survive.

This collection started when my father walked into FAO Schwartz in New York on a pre-Christmas day in 1973, and,

Thus started, we never looked back. We scoured auction houses and antique stores in search of examples from every major toy boat maker and found that many originated from the Nuremburg area of Germany. They were made from the 1870s up to about 1955, with most coming from what is now known as the Golden Age of Toys. We set a few limits, deciding not to include model boats because they were hand built and unique, usually fashioned after an existing ship and certainly not meant to be played with. No plastic either. Nor was condition the top criterion, which surprised many. Our reasoning was simple: this was a toy and was meant to be played with. So if there were dings and dents, paint loss, or burn marks around its steam power plant, it showed the toy had been loved and used and that somehow it had survived to find its way to us. We did pay top dollar a few times for fine, pristine examples of the toy makers' art, so we had a great range of boats for our hunting.

We ended up with about 500 in our fleet, and many are pictured on the pages that follow. All the great firms are represented, with the majority from Germany, a number from the United States, and the rest from France and other countries.

Not all the boats float, as not all children had ponds to play on. So our collection has floor toys made of wood and covered in lithographed paper. Some are cast iron, and there's even a bank. One of my favorites is *L'Amphibo*, a French belle époque dandy from 1906 that can run as a car when wound up or float along as an elegant launch.

So what is it about these toys that still fascinates me? I look on them as a reflection of the world they came from, a world still linked by water: passenger liners carrying immigrants to a new world or the wealthy to visit the old; warships that protected boundaries or helped annex new ones; and pleasure boats that existed for just that, for messing about in boats.

Unlike a toy train that could always have cars added or a doll that needed new outfits, the boat is a complete toy, its world limited only by the imagination of its captain, with the seven seas or a small pond to be conquered. In the toy boat, too, the toy makers' art was complete, with hand-painted details, mechanisms that were the most up-to-date available, and styling that was based on the finest designs of the time, all reflecting a pride in a growing world that was then made available to a child of any age.

In this collection you will see how sailing ships were quickly eclipsed by steamships during the Industrial Revolution and how the toy manufacturers responded with battleships and floating palaces right up to World War I. After the war, attention to detail and lifelike replication became greater, but the toys began to lose a bit of their playfulness and exaggeration. After the Second World War, only a few manufacturers remained and, by the mid 1950s, they had abandoned tin for the new, very flexible plastic. But by then boats had started to give way to planes as the most common form of transportation, and the need for toy boats faded.

For some, though, the lure of boats and water is still vivid. So welcome aboard this good book, and I hope you enjoy your wonderful journey though its pages—with your imagination as your ticket to the world.

L'AMPHIBO

This delightful car boat is an amphibious vehicle designed by a certain Grémillet and exhibited in Paris in 1906. It's crafted of tin and wood and powered by a simple rubber band. **12" long**

THE LAND
OF COUNTERPANE

. . .

BY ROBERT LOUIS STEVENSON (1850–94)

When I was sick and lay a-bed,
    I had two pillows at my head,
And all my toys beside me lay
    To keep me happy all the day.

And sometimes for an hour or so
    I watched my leaden soldiers go,
With different uniforms and drills,
    Among the bed-clothes, through the hills;

And sometimes sent my ships in fleets
    All up and down among the sheets;
Or brought my trees and houses out,
    And planted cities all about.

I was the giant great and still
    That sits upon the pillow-hill,
And sees before him, dale and plain,
    The pleasant land of counterpane.

Land of Counterpane Jessie Wilcox Smith oil and charcoal on board **22" x 14"**

A U T O M A T I C   R O W E R

French **22½" long**

A U T O M A T E D   R O W B O A T S

(left) **D.R. Patent** wood **20" long**; (right) tin **10¾" long**

P U L L   T O Y   R O W B O A T   W I T H   C R E W

American Mechanical Toy Co. **14" long**

CHAPTER 1:

THE BIRTH AND GROWTH OF A GRAND COLLECTION

"THE THINGS OF CHILDHOOD HAVE A LASTING IMPRESSION
THROUGHOUT ONE'S LIFE. IF THEY ARE PLAY-WITH-ABLE,
IMAGINATIVE, AND BEAUTIFUL, IT'S IMPORTANT."

—Malcolm Forbes

Why in the world would a busy, successful publisher—with an extremely active recreational and social life—ever decide to amass what is probably the single most important and valuable collection of antique toy boats in the world?

Blame his father.

The collector—who also accumulated Fabergé and toy soldiers—was, of course, Malcolm Forbes. And his father, the man who founded *Forbes* magazine in 1917, was Bertie Charles (B.C.) Forbes.

Coming to America as a young man with very little money, B.C. Forbes made his way into the circle of prominent New York businessmen. He became the best-known financial columnist of his day before starting his own magazine that catapulted him into legendary status as a pioneer of business-oriented journalism.

B.C. Forbes once said, "Business was originated to produce happiness not to pile up millions." And he passed on to his sons a zest for life that went well beyond the desire to make money.

He also gave them a family tradition that made a lasting impression. The family would periodically travel back to Scotland, the "homeland," by boat. And B.C. Forbes would buy toy boats—especially yachts—for his five sons, including Malcolm. On one ocean voyage, the young Malcolm lowered a toy boat into the sea so that it, too, could cross the Atlantic. Needless to say, it quickly sank beneath the waves, and was never seen again. In "My Fantasy Fleet," an article he wrote for *Art & Antiques* magazine, July 19, 1989, Malcolm said of this lost boat:

"Many of us have a Rosebud lurking in our past—a toy train, a truck, a doll, or like Citizen Kane, a sled. For me, it was a little toy boat that slid to a watery grave somewhere on the floor of the Atlantic, its captain's spirit going down with the ship. I've commanded plenty of toy boats in my time, and sank more than a few, but of all the helms I've lost, that one looms largest."

In the foreword to the book *Toy Boats 1870–1955: A Pictorial History*, co-written by his son Robert, Malcolm Forbes said:

"Boats and the sea always had strong appeal for me. The first time I sailed on an ocean monarch was at the age of seven, aboard the *Aquitania*. My Scotland-born father loved to revisit the Aberdeenshire scenes of his youth and so most every other summer until World War II our family sailed to

Portrait of the Malcolm Forbes Family John Koch oil on canvas 1956 **24½" x 34"**

IVES SINGLE OARSMAN BOAT CARRIE

The *Carrie* is also known as the "Warner single oarsman" after its inventor, Nathan S. Warner. This clockwork toy—distinguished by the very realistic movement of the oarsman—was patented by Warner in 1869. **10½" long**

BRASS BOAT WITH STEAM ENGINE
Buckman c.1890 **12½" long**

Southampton, or sometimes directly to Glasgow by the Anchor Line. After Scotland, we would go to Europe and sail home from Le Havre or Marseilles."

The memories of those dreamy voyages—and the joy and jubilation of playing with those masterful boats—never ceased to stir the heart, soul, and imagination of the ever-energetic Malcolm Forbes. But it would be many years into his career before Malcolm Forbes began his astonishing toy boat collection.

Meanwhile, this man was a twice-decorated war hero, author, state senator, balloonist, and Harley-Davidson® enthusiast. After roughly a decade in politics, Malcolm turned his attention to *Forbes* magazine and injected his contagious enthusiasm into the enterprise in the '60s. As sole owner and publisher, he engineered the dramatic expansion of the magazine, which was highly successful and brought Malcolm the wealth he needed to satisfy his appetite for collecting.

But why and when did he start building a collection that would ultimately total 500 toy boats? Malcolm described the fateful day when he started collecting the boats in "My Fantasy Fleet":

"Happily, and perhaps not surprisingly, my own children grew up loving to play with boats. I can't truly say that the collection started with that in mind, however. It started when I spotted an antique toy boat at FAO Schwartz—a fabulous ship of a size I'd never had the means to possess, perhaps thirty inches long, really magnificent—and I bought it for quite a large sum. Soon after, at an auction . . . a few tin boats showed up, and I couldn't resist buying them."

That was in 1973. That first toy boat was an ocean liner made by the firm of Joseph Falk of Nuremberg, Germany, one of the many great toy boat manufacturers to be discussed later in this book (see especially Chapter 4). As Forbes acknowledges, that first acquisition quickly led to hundreds more. The Forbes' and their co-conspirators would conspire to acquire the toy boats they prized from auctions, flea markets, dealers, and individual collectors.

FROM PLAYROOM TO SHOWROOM...
FROM TOYS TO TREASURES

As Malcolm Forbes began to accumulate more and more toy boats, he found that the shelf space in the kids' playroom could no longer hold his burgeoning collection. But that didn't stop him. He kept buying more and more boats and often joined his boys as they played with these precious treasures in the Forbes pool and pond. Then Malcolm realized that, with the steadily higher prices he was paying for these increasingly rare antiques, they could no longer be considered mere toys. It dawned on him that he was now a bona fide collector.

Malcolm and his son Robert built the Forbes toy boat

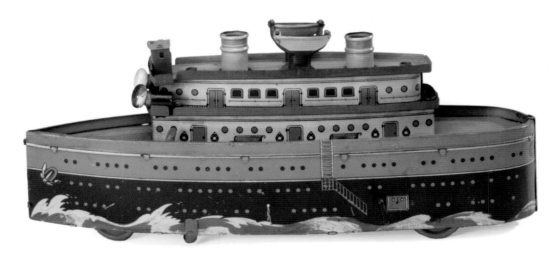

PAINTED TINPLATE BOAT

This twin-funneled, hand-painted tinplate boat runs on a clockwork mechanism wound by a handle at the rear. The mechanism activates the three-bladed propeller. Finished overall in cream with red, green, and brown detailing. Made in Germany. c. 1920 **8¼" long**

*(excerpts from "My Fantasy Fleet," written by Malcolm Forbes
for* Art & Antiques *magazine)*

I cannot pinpoint exactly when this fascination with boats began, but my earliest memories are of being totally engrossed in the bathtub with what were called in those days "talcum tugs." I used to go to the medicine cabinet and take the lids off all the containers big enough to float. Then, making waves, I'd imagine storms at sea and log which of my makeshift armada stayed afloat the longest.

Early on I started asking for toy boats for Christmas, birthdays, or Easter.

Toy boats were quite expensive, everything being relative, but with the smaller ones of six, eight, ten, or twelve inches I could play for hours on the rug, dreaming I was sailing the oceans of the world. As much as I loved toy boats when I was a kid, I didn't collect them. I *played* with them. But it's clear to me that it was nostalgia more than anything else that sparked both the toy boat and the toy soldier collections—the warm, embracing memories of the endless fun we had with them.

About a half a mile from our house on the outskirts of Englewood, New Jersey, there were . . . Englewood Cliffs. At its base ran a busy brook. There my brothers and I would launch our little tin ocean liners and let the current take them along while we followed. When they'd encounter branches or obstacles, or the water was too strong, one of the boats might capsize and sink, and then we'd have to decide whether we were going to make a major disaster of it and mourn the drowned or retrieve it, shake it out, and continue as if nothing had happened. Barring tragedies, the longest voyage the boats could make without portage was to the Devil's Hole, our local swimming hole. For our tiny navy, that was the end of the line.

Perhaps one reason my brothers and I were so obsessed with boats was that from a very early age we were lucky enough to cruise with our parents on some of the great old four-stack liners. Almost every other summer until World War II, our family would sail to Great Britain, oft times directly to Glasgow on the Anchor Line, other times to Southampton via Cunard or White Star. From Scotland we would go to Europe, and we'd sail home from Le Havre or Marseilles.

On one crossing I took a toy boat and, with my brother's aid, lowered it—secured by a strong twine—the long way from rail to sea. We intended that this toy liner too should make the Atlantic crossing. It survived departure from the dock, but within a few minutes . . . the bashing soon saw it underway to Davey Jones's locker. On the return trip, we decided we'd raise our spirits with a little conspiratorial fun: creating the impression that the entire liner had sunk. We found items with the ship's name on them—life preservers, pillows, anything that would float—and stuffed the whole lot out the porthole. We figured a passing ship would recover them and think the *President Hayes* had gone to the bottom. But it was *our* bottoms that suffered. When the stewards took inventory at the end of the trip, they noticed all the missing items and discussed our seagoing deportment with our parents. In addition to spankings, our modest allowances were encumbered until accounts were settled to the Dollar Line's satisfaction. And our little boat was lost, but in spirit it may have led to the start of my fantasy fleet.

CAST-IRON SIDEWHEELERS

(from top to bottom) Wilkins **Puritan** 10¾" long; Wilkins **City of New York** 15½" long; Dent **Adirondack** 14½" long

BING FERRY BOAT

22½" long

IVES RIVERBOAT SALLY

Like Samuel Orkin's company, the Ives Manufacturing Corporation made it their business to try to entice young men to join the U.S. Merchant Marine. But this is just a charming, little hand-painted riverboat that used to chug along powered by a key-wound clockwork mechanism. c. 1923 **10½" long**

collection together. Some boats were purchased at auction, sometimes for record-breaking prices. Within a decade, father and son had accumulated more than 500 antique toy boats, including ocean liners, warships, submarines, riverboats, speedboats, and rowboats from auctions, flea markets, dealers, and fellow collectors. In "Capitalist Toys: A Selection of Toy Boats and Toy Motorcycles" from *The Forbes Magazine Collection*, a booklet published for the Sotheby's auction of December 19, 1994, Malcolm said of his son Robert: ". . . he has had as much fun as his father assembling this collection, and he has brought to it a knowledge of the subject and scope that I never had." And Robert said, "While Pop loved the ocean liners, I went for battleships, and together we fleshed out the other categories."

How did the Forbeses find so many hard-to-find treasures? They ran ads in publications like *Antique Toy World* magazine and purchased antique toy boats from people who responded to their ads. Dealers and individual collectors often sent letters and photos of their cherished toy boats to Malcolm and Robert, who bought the ones they wanted. The Forbeses were intimately involved, and mutually decided on

all the acquisitions.

"We made many trips together to visit auctions, collectors, and dealers, bargained hard, and often bought on the spot," said Robert Forbes. "Once we became known as boat buyers, the inevitable dilemma presented itself: we were usually the first to be called when someone decided to sell, but this privilege meant we were usually given the highest price. Though some may have thought that they bested us, as times and prices rolled on, the only real regrets we had were boats not bought" ("Capitalist Toys," 1994).

After living his life with unabashed gusto and sheer joy, Malcolm Forbes passed away on February 24, 1990. Fortunately, before he died, Malcolm had engineered one of his greatest accomplishments: the Forbes Galleries, which had opened five years before, in 1985. As the story goes, Malcolm walked into the *Forbes* magazine building and declared that the entire first floor would be used for his collections. The collections are there to this very day, and all are welcome to see them. Admission is free.

Today, Robert Forbes, and many people within the Forbes Galleries, carry on Malcolm's legacy.

EARLY FRENCH PADDLE-DRIVEN PASSENGER BOAT

This toy boat exudes French charm with its yellow-and-white striped awning, blue-and-white smokestack, ornate fleur-de-lis design on the sides, front and back, and the intricate design with the romantic heart motif in center of each side. Complete with stand. **20½" long**

MÄRKLIN NEW YORK

Crafted in 1904, this intricate toy boat was housed in a museum for years, which helped to keep it in good condition. Unfortunately, to make it fit on a shelf in the museum, components were removed and subsequently lost. The passengers and tiny oars are original, whereas the masts and rigging were replaced. The *New York* is crafted of hand-painted tin with a cast-iron walk beam. It sports two ventilators, two side wheels, lifeboats, and an American flag in front. The side-wheel covers were painted with *New York*, a common theme in toy boats of the era. The German manufacturers—including Märklin—decorated a toy boat with a name of a city or country to make it more appealing to a national or local market. **31½" long**

MÄRKLIN ST. MALO RIVERBOAT

Perhaps named for the river town in Brittany, France where ferries still run regularly. **17" long**

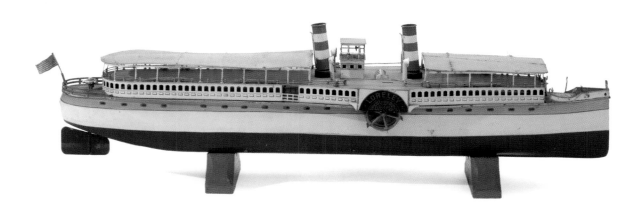

MÄRKLIN CLOCKWORK PADDLE STEAMER LORELEY

This toy boat was acquired through David Pressland, a friend of the Forbes family and a collecting expert. A friend of Pressland's was selling it. Reminiscent of the paddle steamers that would cruise leisurely down the Rhine or the Danube in Europe, the *Loreley* is distinguished by the most remarkable detailing, including dozens of windows. **30" long**

BING BATTLESHIP TERRIBLE

Both Bing and Märklin created toy ships named *Terrible*, and both were crafted to appeal to the English market. This Bing model, however, is more accurate. Like many models of ships, its name derived from a full-sized ship in active service. It was modeled after *SM Linienschiff Brandenburg* of the Imperial German Navy. Oddly enough, in Bing's 1902 catalog, this ship bears the title *Worth*, and the name *Brandenburg* appears with another ship. A metal casting was used to simulate the gold decoration around the bows. **29½" long**

CHAPTER 2

WELCOME TO "SHIPS AHOY!" IN THE HEART OF THE FORBES GALLERIES

"Now, just pretend it's some years back, before TV and even before the airplane, and think about what these boats meant to those generations of ageless children."

—Robert L. Forbes

More than 60,000 people visit the Forbes Galleries on Fifth Avenue in New York City annually. If you should venture into the "Ships Ahoy!" section of the Forbes Galleries, you will see eight gold, ground glass panels that were designed by Jean Dupas (1882–1964) for the Grand Salon of the *Normandie*. The mirrorlike brilliance of these panels has been achieved through an unusual technique: the scenes were painted on the reverse of the panels of plate glass, after which gold and silver leaf was applied, a process known as *verre églomisé*.

The boats in the Forbes Galleries span the spectrum—ranging from elegant antiques of the late nineteenth to the mid-twentieth century. This trove of nautical treasure glimmers and shimmers with the finest achievements of the great toy boat makers, including Märklin, Bing, Fleischmann, and Carette. The pleasure boats include *L'Amphibo*, a delightful car boat. The handsomely preserved, richly detailed ocean liners make one want to cruise to Europe, as Malcolm and his brothers often did. The paddlewheel boats evoke Mark Twain's accounts of Huck Finn exploring the Mississippi. And any child—and many an adult—would love to get his hands on one of the perfectly equipped battleships and fire a tiny brass cannon.

THEY ARE THE RAREST OF ANTIQUE TOYS BECAUSE
THEY FULFILLED THEIR PURPOSE—THEY WERE PLAYED WITH

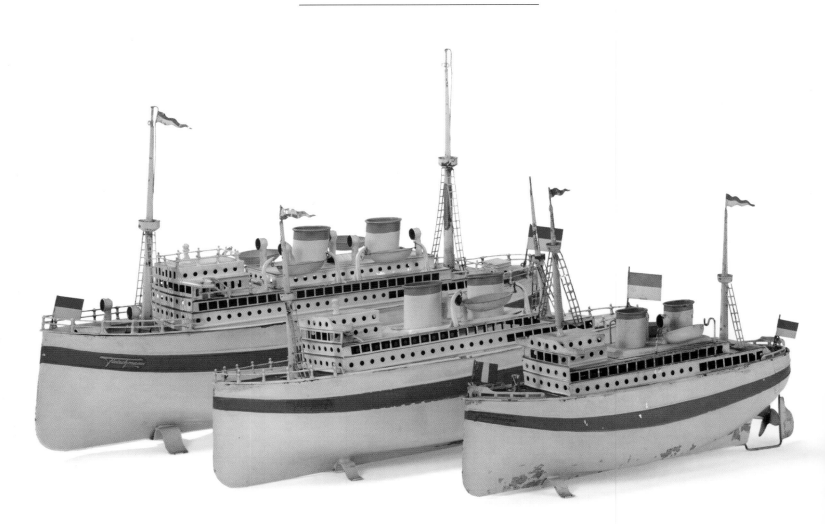

FLEISCHMANN ALBERT BALLIN OCEAN LINERS
c. 1955 (from left to right) **19½"; 17"; 13½" long**

FLEISCHMANN OCEAN LINER
C. 1910 **24" long**

THESE ARE TOYS,
NOT MODELS

"What exactly is a toy boat?" asks a signboard on a glass display case housing the Forbes flotilla of warships. The text on the sign-board explains that, unlike models that were crafted one at a time for collectors, toy boats were mass-produced. While collector models were highly intricate replicas of real ships, the emphasis with toys was on playability rather than realism. "Powered by steam, battery or clockwork, toy boats had a tough life. They blew up, sank, forgot to come back or just rusted away, leaving few survivors. They are the rarest of antique toys because they fulfilled their purpose—they were played with."

"The difference between a toy boat and a model boat is that a model is unique, hand-built, fashioned after an existing ship, and not meant to be played with," Robert Forbes once said. "But that's not to say there's no detailing on toy boats. In the early years of manufacturing, great attention was paid to the paint jobs, railings, lifeboats, and guns. What added to the 'fun-ness' . . . was that these details were exaggerated and

emphasized rather than just being made to scale."

The toy boats Forbes is referring to came out between 1870 and 1950. Many were produced during the golden age of toy boats, which began in roughly 1870 and continued in the early twentieth century before coming to a halt with the Great War.

It all started in Nuremberg, Germany.

The heyday of toy boats was around 1900, and its center was Nuremberg, Germany. The now famous Nuremberg toy makers—including Märklin and Bing—made toy boats inspired by the great ocean liners of that glorious era. These toy boats found their way into the homes of children throughout Europe and the Americas.

The toy makers knew that the magnificent ships that sailed the seven seas during the early 1900s captivated people's imaginations. Children who had never seen the full-size vessels could be enthralled by their grandeur, handsomely captured in toy boats crafted to the highest standards of the toy maker's art. Soon lakes, ponds, and bathtubs were ruled by youthful sailors with their majestic tin boats.

Just as the children of a bygone era could imagine being the captain and crew of a grand ocean liner as they watched their toy boats course through the water, they could also picture themselves sailing across—or below—the waters in a war to preserve liberty. As the romance of leisurely ocean travel gave way to thoughts of war early in the twentieth century, the toy makers responded to the desire for military vessels by making toy battleships and submarines.

THE TOY MAKERS ACT
ON THE RUMBLINGS OF WAR

The warships usually featured miniature toy guns. Some of these guns could actually be loaded with gunpowder and fired, adding to the drama. Some even featured delayed-action firing, meaning the guns fired after a specific time lapse, which made the explosions all the more dramatic. For added realism and drama, toy boat enthusiasts bought small cannons to set up at the edge of the water. These cannons could actually fire at the toy boats sailing nearby.

Submarines were not only capable of traveling beneath the water, but some could fire torpedoes. The Forbes Galleries of toy boats house many of these functional military ships and subs. The key to making a good toy submarine was to engineer a control mechanism that would enable the sub to resurface. In one of the more popular systems, hydrofoils or fins were fitted to the hull. When the spring was fully wound, the clockwork motor propelled the boat under water. Then, when the motor ran down, the sub's buoyancy brought it back to the surface.

Märklin made submarines in which the clockwork altered the hydrofoil setting with a system of levers. The sub could dive and resurface several times with just one winding. Plank utilized a small trolley that carried a lead weight; the trolley moved back and forth as the clockwork motor turned. This adjusted the sub's trim in accordance with the position of the weight, which caused the vessel to rise or sink.

The system that most closely resembled a full-size submarine was based on chemical action. The toy U-boat was equipped with ballast tanks, just like a real sub. Baking soda or a similar powder was dumped into the tanks, and the toy

MÄRKLIN SUBMARINE

This Märklin submarine is a wonder. When wound up with its key, it shoots along the surface and dives again and resurfaces, just like a real submarine. You can have no end of fun with it as it attacks wooden ships that you make for your war game. **10" long**

ANDRE THE GIANT

All in all, the "Ships Ahoy!" collection is pretty evenly divided between ocean liners and warships. Crafted of cast iron, the *Andre* is the largest toy vessel in the collection. It is an extraordinary replica of a nineteenth century battleship distinguished by a gas-powered engine and intricate details in zinc and bronze. It was acquired from the Nain-Jaune store in Paris. **47" long**

CAST-IRON BELLBOAT **LANDING OF COLUMBUS**
J & E Stevens **7" long**

FRENCH TIN PULL TOY
19th century **8½" long**

sub was launched. When water came into the tanks, the sub dove. When the water reached the powder, gases were created through a chemical reaction that blew the water from the tanks. When the sub had lost the weight of the water, it rose again to the surface.

HOW DID THEY MAKE THESE TOYS GO?

Most of the toy boats in the Forbes collection ran on clockwork mechanisms. For these, there is generally a key extending from the smokestack, sometimes designed to look like a cloud of smoke. Kids of previous generations turned the key to wind the spring inside. When the key was removed, the spring unwound, and the boat would move forward. The clockwork mechanisms that propelled these valiant vessels were the most economi-

cal and the simplest and safest for a child to operate.

The toy boats in the "Ships Ahoy!" collection are mostly crafted of tin, which was inexpensive and yet provided an excellent medium for paint and lithography. Also, tin watercraft were simply more seaworthy than cast-iron and wooden boats.

While the German companies dominated the field of tin toy boats, the Americans distinguished themselves in the manufacture of cast-iron toys produced from molds that could be reused, creating great efficiencies. Many of the cast-iron toys were of the pull-type variety.

"Not all the boats float," says Robert Forbes, "as not all children had ponds to play with. So our collection has floor toys made out of wood with lithographed paper on it, and other non-floaters like 'Walbert Ferry.'"

Moreover, while the great toy boat makers responded to the appetite for ocean liners and military vessels, they also

A PERSONAL STORY

How personal can the experience of seeing the Forbes collection of toy boats be? In February of 1980, a Forbes employee by the name of Vera Vent visited the Forbes Galleries and then wrote a letter to Malcolm Forbes. Here are excerpts:

I can't begin to tell you what a surprise and thrill it was to find a model of the U.S.S. *Leviathan* in your collection of toy boats.

This is the boat that brought my mother and me to America from France in March, 1927. As you probably know, it was originally *The Fatherland*, a German vessel. It was acquired by the United States Lines as part of the war reparations after World War I. My Dad was chief of the Detroit office of the US Lines at that time, after spending some years in Russia with the American Relief Administration under Hoover. He met and married my mother there and was able to get her, her mother and two sisters out of Russia. They settled in Meudon, a suburb of Paris, and a year later, I was born in Neuilly in the American Hospital. Subsequently, Dad felt he had spent enough time in Europe and that it was time for him to return home. He got the job with the US Lines and that's how we came to make our crossing on the *Leviathan*.

BING LEVIATHAN

The name *Leviathan* is not only perfectly suited to the original ocean liner, but it's an apt appellation for this toy boat as well. Over three feet from bow to stern, it weighs a whopping twelve pounds. Purchased by the Forbeses for the collection in 1974 for a mere $3,000, this hand-painted tin toy made the cover of *Toy Boats 1870–1955: A Pictorial History*, co-written by Robert Forbes. A twin screw boat with a heavy spring that requires a crank to wind it, this craft is propelled by a clockwork mechanism. Its elaborate details include twelve life rafts, three stacks, and three masts. **39¾" long**

27

Z I P P - E E

10¾" long

found a receptive consumer audience with more whimsical creations. Among these was an American-made *Zipp-ee* speedboat powered by a balloon attached to a tube emerging from the boat's stern.

In the Forbes collection, there is also the tin *L'Amphibo* boat-on-wheels, propelled by a rubber band. This creation won a French toy inventors' contest in 1906. The Forbes flotilla of toy boats also showcases sailboats with paper, cloth, and tin sails. There's even a toy boat transformed into a lamp with a clear bulb revealing a glowing filament in the shape of the ever-courageous Popeye the Sailor.

THEY DON'T MAKE TOYS LIKE THIS ANYMORE

While they were originally purchased as toys, many of the boats in the Forbes collection are truly museum-quality masterpieces. Many are extremely rare and highly valuable, and some are literally one-of-a-kind. Earlier lithographed tin boats were often not made to float and were provided with wheels. They were either made as pulltoys or powered by a spring motor. These, too, can be found in the "Ships Ahoy!" collection.

Perhaps the most remarkable quality that so many of the Forbes toy boats have in common is that they were, in fact, toys. In an electronic world filled with PCs, DVDs, and video games, it's hard to imagine a toy maker willing to invest so much ingenuity and workmanship in a mere plaything. And if such toys came out today, few could afford them. As Malcolm Forbes said in "My Fantasy Fleet," "Sadly, no child plays with these toys anymore. They are too fragile and too expensive, so most of them are locked up in collections like ours. Still, it would be a melancholy affair to look at toy boats by yourself, so the Forbes armada remains anchored in our galleries at Fifth Avenue and Twelfth Street in New York." Forbes also revealed perhaps his most compelling motivation for exposing the "Ships Ahoy!" collection to the public. "Sharing the fun of these boats with future generations of bathtub admirals is almost as pleasurable, for me, as remembering how it all began."

The only way to understand fully what Forbes meant is to plan a trip to the Forbes Galleries in New York City.

MÄRKLIN OLYMPIA

Built at Union Iron Works, San Francisco, California, and launched on November 5, 1892, the U.S.S. *Olympia* was the oldest steel-hulled American warship afloat when it served as Commodore George Dewey's flagship during the Battle of Manila Bay on May 1, 1898. Dewey and his troops dealt the Spanish naval forces in the Philippines a crushing defeat, securing the Philippines for the United States. The cruiser was the product of a program of ships for the "New Navy" of the late nineteenth century. Designed to correct the deficiencies of an inferior naval force, the program led to the rise of the steel shipbuilding industry in the United States. *Olympia* is the last remaining ship built during that program and the sole surviving naval warship of the Spanish-American War. It served as the training vessel for the U.S. Naval Academy until 1909, was reactivated for World War I, and took part in the Allied landings in Murmansk in 1918. *Olympia*'s last major mission was the return of the Unknown Soldier from Europe after World War I for reburial in Arlington National Cemetery. Today U.S.S. *Olympia* is a National Historic Landmark berthed in Philadelphia, Pennsylvania. And the toy boat produced by Märklin so long ago pays tribute to this famous vessel. Sculpted in front to capture the hand-carved bow of a great warship, this masterful toy came complete with cannons on the deck and intricate rigging. **17" long**

BING SAILBOAT **DEFENDER**

This hand-painted sailboat with cloth sails is complete with stand. **21½" long**

MINT RADIGUET STEAM-DRIVEN YACHT

Zinc hull, wood deck and masts. Sculpted detail on front. Anchor on side. **16" long**

MÄRKLIN CLOCKWORK FRIGATE **MARTHA**

A clipper ship, dating from before the age of the great ocean liners, this is a very rare toy boat, handsomely crafted with cloth sails. Note it also has a clockwork engine for days with no wind. **28" long**

CHAPTER 3

FROM THE LUSITANIA TO THE MISSOURI, TOY BOATS REFLECT THE TIMES

"LOOK ON THESE TOYS AS A REFLECTION OF
THE WORLD THEY CAME FROM..."

—Robert L. Forbes

In his introduction to this book, Robert Forbes writes . . . "look on [these toys] as a reflection of the world they came from, a world still linked by water: passenger liners carrying immigrants to a new world or the wealthy to visit the old; warships that protected boundaries or helped annex new ones; and pleasure boats that existed for just that, for messing about in boats."

In the nineteenth and early twentieth century, social and historical trends and events often influenced the design of toys. As the Industrial Revolution came into full swing, sailing ships gave way to steamships. Initially, in the 1830s and later, the early steamships often met tragic fates, the most dramatic example being the *Titanic* in 1912. But ocean liners quickly improved and attracted more and more passen-

gers. The *Mauretania* and *Lusitania* could take thousands of people across the Atlantic in less than a week. But speed and size were just part of the romance of these great ships. They were appointed with so many amenities that they rivaled the great hotels of Europe.

In step with the changing times, the toy manufacturers responded with mighty steam-powered battleships and battery-powered floating palaces like the *Lusitania*, which captured the pride and joy of the famed Cunard shipping line. These mass-produced tinplate and cast-iron toys were often given by parents as Christmas and birthday gifts to children in America and other countries between the Civil War and World War I. The products of a recently industrialized and increasingly mechanized society, these metal toys were the

CHILDREN WHO HAD NEVER SEEN THE FULL-SIZE VESSELS

COULD BE ENTHRALLED BY THEIR GRANDEUR

MÄRKLIN MAURETANIA

This very fine, three-funnel ocean liner is distinguished by its original paint, stand, and American and Märklin logo flags. There are a total of five replacement lifeboats. The key on top is for winding the clockwork mechanism inside. **21½" long**

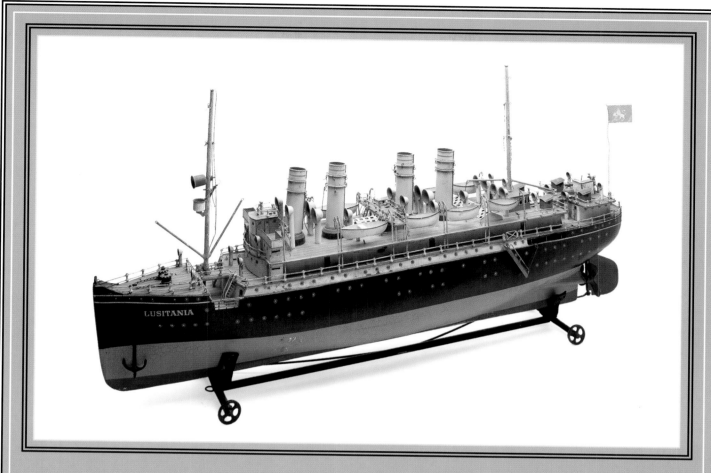

MÄRKLIN LUSITANIA

The heart and soul of the famed Cunard shipping line, the *Lusitania* was built in 1907. On May 17, 1915, a German submarine sank the ship, precipitating U.S. entry into World War I. Märklin's magnificent hand-painted tin, electric-powered toy became the property of Malcolm Forbes for $28,600 at Sotheby's New York auction, which wasn't the first time a Forbes broke the record for the highest price ever paid for a toy boat.

Prior to the Sotheby's auction, the auction house ran an ad in the January 1983 issue of *Antique Toy World* showing the *Lusitania* and promoting their "Collector's Carousel" auctions. The toy was delivered to Sotheby's by Pamela Brown Sherer, Sotheby's collectibles expert, who acquired it from a woman in Pennsylvania. Because of its value (estimated at a mere $8,000 to $12,000 prior to the auction), Sherer personally transported the *Lusitania* by cab all the way to New York. (Her cab fare was a whopping $140.)

This toy boat is a reflection of both Cunard's and Märklin's scrupulous attention to detail. Notice the equidistant stacks, a hallmark of Cunard's symmetry in design. A full 37½" in length, this "toy" is a masterpiece, complete with two lead seamen and a seated passenger. From the bell on the front mast to the five pairs of lifeboats, the *Lusitania* is distinguished by the rich detailing that made Märklin the undisputed leader in toy boats. The decks are fitted with a bridge and four funnels, two masts, two capstans with anchors forward, and a ship's wheel that controls the rudder aft of twin propellers. The red flag flying above bears a rampant lion holding a globe. Stamped with the Märklin mark on the rudder, the *Lusitania* rests on its original wheeled base.

In the "Ships Ahoy!" collection in the Forbes Galleries, the fate of the *Lusitania* is dramatically depicted in an undersea world thick with submarines.

ultimate reflection of progress. Just as horse-drawn vehicles gave way to the automotive age, and people left farms to work in cities, the handcrafted wooden toys of the first half of the nineteenth century were succeeded by toys made of metal.

BUT WHAT KIND OF TOYS WERE THEY?

As passenger trade became more lucrative, the builders of great European ocean liners competed more aggressively with each other, most notably in England, Germany, and France. And this spirited rivalry gave the world such splendid vessels as the *Titanic* and *Kaiserin Augusta Victoria*. The great liners were symbols of national pride and industrial might.

As always, the toy makers kept their fingers on the pulse of the times. The golden age of the ocean liner produced the heyday of toy boats. Just as the big boat builders vied with each other for prominence, the toy makers tried to outdo one another. But it was the Nuremberg firm of Märklin that ruled the waters where toy boats were found. Märklin's many marvelous creations included three that ultimately found their way into the Forbes Galleries: the stunning *Kaiserin Augusta Victoria*, just under four feet in length, the *Baltimore*, some 30 inches long, and the aforementioned *Lusitania*, crafted to glorious proportions by Märklin in 1909.

Be forewarned. If you come to see such beautifully preserved, fully-equipped ocean liners on display in the Forbes Galleries, don't be surprised if you feel the sudden urge to book immediate passage on a cruise to distant destinations.

During the last few decades of the nineteenth century and the early twentieth century, yachting was all the rage, and toy makers responded to the trend with elegant toy yachts. Like many toy boats of the era, these were often schooner-rigged, because a square-rigged toy wouldn't float well. In the 1860s, the world witnessed the transition from

MÄRKLIN KAISERIN AUGUSTA VICTORIA

When she was built for Germany's Hamburg-America Line, *Kaiserin Augusta Victoria* was initially called *Europa* and was the world's largest passenger ship. But when this steamship was launched on August 29, 1905, she was renamed after the wife of the Emperor Wilhelm II. Carrying 593 crew members, she could accommodate 652 passengers in first class, 286 in second class, 216 in third class, and 1,842 in steerage. On her maiden voyage, *Kaiserin Augusta Victoria* traveled from Hamburg, Germany, to Dover, England, on to Cherbourg, France, and ended up in New York City. This ship weighed close to 25,000 tons. At the end of World War I, she underwent transfer to the U.S. Shipping Board for use as a troop transport, and she was later chartered by the Cunard Line. In 1921, the ship was renamed *Empress of Scotland*, but she sank in 1930. The Märklin toy boat is nearly four feet long and richly captures the grandeur of the original—from the three smokestacks to the many lifeboats to the railings. **45" long**

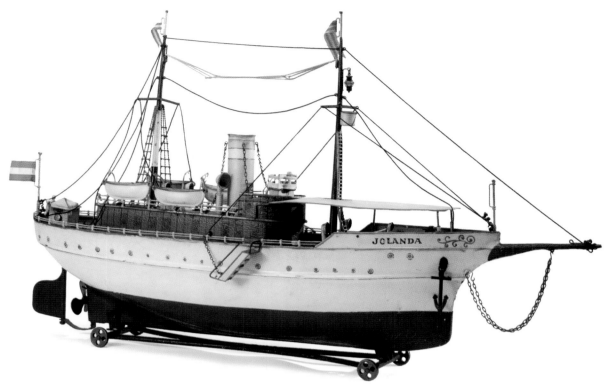

MÄRKLIN **JOLANDA**

Driven by clockwork, this painted tin yacht is crafted with elaborate rigging and lifeboats on the top deck. **19" long**

sail to steam, and many nations' navies and mercantile marine forces began operating in steam-driven vessels.

Right around the turn of the century, motorboat racing became a favorite pastime. One reason for this is that it provided the perfect opportunity to put a new engine to the test. Not surprisingly, the toy makers detected the enthusiasm for motorboats and tapped into the trend with stylish toy boats.

TOYS EVOLVE WITH SHIP TECHNOLOGY AND DESIGN

In the early twentieth century, maritime technology and design advanced at an unparalleled pace. Ocean liners doubled in size and speed. Warships evolved into massive dreadnoughts, and submarines changed the nature of war.

All of these developments were followed closely by the toy boat manufacturers, who made whatever was in vogue. But how did they propel increasingly sophisticated and, consequently, larger toy boats?

Just as steam could power big ships, it was equally effective in toys, though they sometimes overheated and even blew up occasionally. But steam and the clockwork motors enabled toy boats to cope more effectively with poor weather. Assuming that the captain of a toy boat set his rudder properly, the clockwork-driven boat usually returned to its owner. As these toys became more reliable, they also became more popular. Toy shops were filled with paddle steamers, steamships, and a wide variety of other toy boats that captivated generations of young boys and girls.

While the passion for traveling to foreign climes fueled the manufacture of ocean liners and majestic toys, military activity ignited public interest in the vessels that waged war. For example, U.S. naval triumphs over Spain in 1898 played a pivotal role. The rumblings of war also made themselves heard when Japan defeated Russia in 1904. And, in a show of naval superiority, America sent its Great White Fleet around the world in 1908 because of United States interests in the Pacific, and President Theodore Roosevelt wanted to let the Japanese know that those interests would be protected.

As the public grew increasingly fascinated by warships during the era of "gunboat diplomacy," the toy makers turned their attention to creating a variety of militaristic toys. These ranged in scope from small gunboats of eight inches in

MÄRKLIN NEW YORK

Made in 1910, this toy boat is modeled after a warship that later took part in the only naval battle in World War I between the great navies of Great Britain and Germany, the Battle of Jutland. There's a British flag in back and a searchlight and anchor in front. Rowboats are attached to the halyards on the sides. **14" long**

BING FUJI

This dreadnought has two guns in the turret in front. There are two smokestacks with a chain from one stack to the other. Note the intricate, full railing. **20" long**

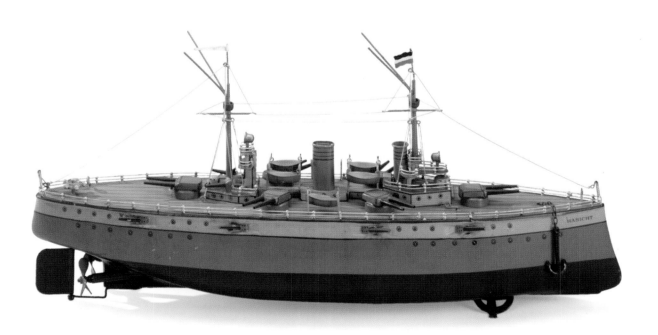

MÄRKLIN HABICHT

This boat is a prime example of Märklin's ability to create toys that were—like the full-size warships—larger than life. It is equipped with multiple, two-gun turrets on deck and four more guns on each side (eight in all) protruding from below deck. Crafted with two smokestacks, two masts, an anchor on the side, and a propeller in back. **20½" long**

length to stately battleships nearly four feet long. These toy military vessels were often equipped with miniature versions of the armament that made the real ships so potent, including turrets that revolved and cannons that fired.

The toy makers' creations reflected the evolution of warship design, especially as naval architecture advanced from the Spanish-American War to the Russo-Japanese War to French and British conquests of far-flung colonies. For example, the projecting prow used to ram an enemy's hull disappeared, and the naval gun gradually ascended from the hull to the deck to the turret.

MILITARY INTERVENTION IN THE TOY BUSINESS

While the development of toy warships came in response to consumer trends, it sometimes benefited from those who had a vested interest in a pro-war mentality. At the turn of the century, the militant German government encouraged production of military-related toys. In fact, in 1898, it did something that would be politically incorrect today. It had the temerity to place newspaper ads extolling the manufacture of war toys.

But perhaps the most remarkable example of the German military's meddling in the affairs of toy companies came in 1913. According to a Berlin newspaper account, the German Kaiser walked into a store and noticed that there weren't any toy submarines for sale. The Kaiser allegedly told the store's clerk, "It is necessary that young Germans understand well that the German maritime strength is invincible, and that the future lies not only on but under the water." He was right, of course. Some 5,000 Allied ships fell to U-boats in the course of World War I. Ironically, their success brought about Germany's defeat. As more and more Americans got killed, America inched closer to entering the war, finally committing to the conflict in April 1917.

Returning to the Kaiser, his enthusiasm and resolve impressed the Nuremberg toy boat makers. They went to work creating warships and submarines. As usual, Märklin led the way with hand-painted cruisers and gunboats. Märklin produced both small and large vessels, ranging from less than a foot to several feet in length.

MÄRKLIN BATTLESHIP **MISSOURI**

Crafted in 1933, this tin toy replica of the famous battleship is driven by a classic clockwork mechanism concealed within the olive green and brown hull. Its two funnels are flanked by twin masts, and the deck detailing includes six revolving, double gun turrets, ten single stationary guns, six lifeboats (with two on davits), walkways, spotlights, working launches, winches, twin propellers, and a five-pointed ship's wheel that controls the rudder. The *Missouri* is stamped in red with the maker's insignia. **28" long**

MÄRKLIN **POSEN**

This highly prized, tin toy boat came back to America with a soldier's possessions after his death in France in 1918. And the Forbeses' $20,000 purchase of this toy warship enabled the Penn State student that owned it to pay his tuition. It bears an intricate motif sculpted in front, an embellishment often found on ships—and toy boats—of the era. Propelled by a battery-powered electric motor, it's equipped with two props, working guns, and lights. The anchors go up and down, and the tiny lifeboats can be mechanically lowered into the water and tied to the sides. And there is a trio of jaunty sailors on deck. **41" long**

BATTLESHIP NEW YORK

Crafted in the late 1890s, this is the largest nickel-plated, cast-iron toy ship ever made. It was made by the Dent Hardware Co. of Pennsylvania. **20" long**

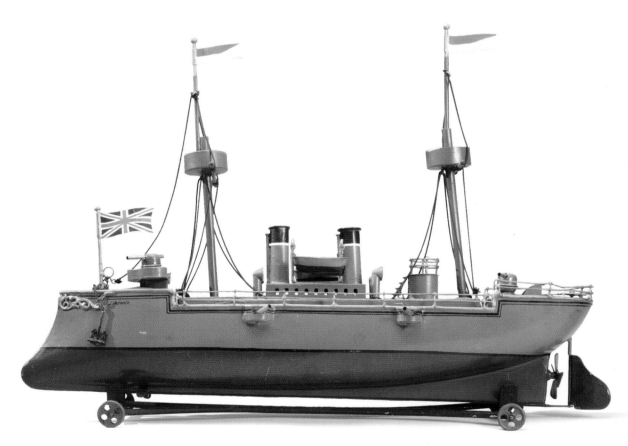

BING BATTLESHIP L'ANTONIO

The Union Jack flutters above a sculpted bow reminiscent of the hand-carved decoration on the ships of a bygone era. Powered by a steam engine, this battleship was crafted with guns on deck, two smokestacks, and twin masts with streamers on top. The intricate detailing includes lustrous, gold-tone railings. **22" long**

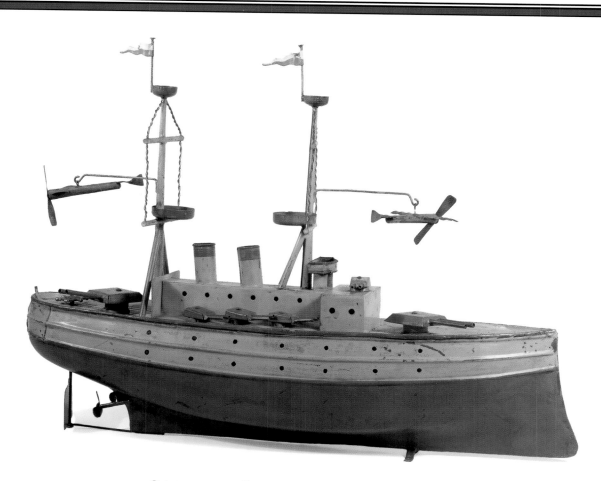

CARETTE GUNBOAT WITH PLANES

Made in 1914, this toy warship boasts two masts—each with a suspended plane—two funnels, nine revolving, double gun turrets, a six-pointed ship's wheel controlling the rudder, and twin propellers. The clockwork mechanism is cleverly concealed within the light blue and ocean blue painted hull. **17" long**

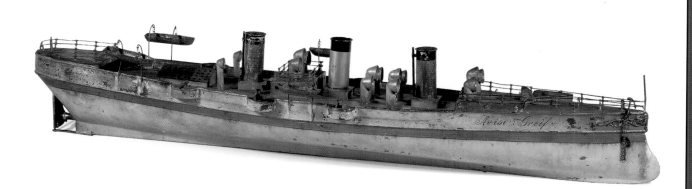

SCHOENNER *AVISO GREIF*

Made in 1900, this sleek and beautifully proportioned painted tin vessel is intricately crafted with three gun turrets, four lifeboats, three smokestacks, two masts, an anchor pire, a gun port on the left side section of starboard, and a quarterdeck lifeline stanchion. This painted tin boat was powered by a wind-up key clockwork mechanism. **28" long**

Märklin's second series of warships included torpedo boats equipped with guns, lifeboats, and crews. The firm offered steam engines for the first time in its illustrious history. Moreover, the company's cruisers were equipped with as many as ten guns and marvelous features like battery-operated spotlights and working semaphore flags. For its third series—from 1918 to 1936—Märklin gave the world handsomely detailed replicas of the legendary battleships of the era. Then the firm concentrated on submarines until World War II.

AN AMERICAN OPPORTUNITY

Another interesting development in the toy industry came about during World War I. The U.S. ceased importing toy boats from Europe, which opened the door for American manufacturers to make some head-way. One of these was Orkin Toys. Samuel Orkin developed an exceptional line of American warships unlike anything made in Europe. His mission was to instill in young boys the values of the post-World War I era as embodied by the merchant marines.

Available at remarkably affordable prices, Orkin's toys were characteristic of the era. However, once World War I was over and the imports of foreign toys resumed, Orkin faced stiff competition. As good as Orkin's boats were, no company outside of Germany seemed to be able to achieve the level of detail and quality that distinguished firms like Märklin and Bing, whose achievements will come across in the next chapter.

When the U.S. entered World War I, the big ocean liners were converted to troop ships to carry our doughboys overseas. In fact, it has been said that these makeshift troop ships

JAPANESE GUNBOAT

Perhaps the most colorful "novelty" boat in the Forbes collection, this spring-wound gunboat is crafted of tin, and its surface is distinguished by a lithographed floral design. Made in 1904 to celebrate Japan's naval victory over Russia, it's decorated with whimsical American flags. This is the type of tin lithographed toy that was once scorned by collectors, but is now highly valued and hard to find. **11" long**

MÄRKLIN WEISSENBERG

When it was purchased in 1979 for $21,000 at PB Eighty-Four at Sotheby's New York, the hand-painted tin boat *Weissenberg* set an all-time price record for a toy boat sold at an auction. Made in 1905, this masterful toy boat is equipped with a key-wound, clockwork mechanism that drove a four-blade propeller. The many authentic details include an anchor and winch, and the rudder is adjusted by an eight-pointed ship's wheel. There are four lifeboats on davits and a bow with cast decoration, as well as a bridge, cannons, gun turrets, twin funnels, and masts surmounted by star-spangled banners. They are finished in hand-painted gray with white handrails and black wheeled support. In a March 1980 article in *Antiques World*, Robert Forbes said, "The boat has wonderful exaggerations. The oversize portholes, large crow's nest, and bulbous gun turrets serve to emphasize the boat's playability." **34½" long**

ORKIN NEVADA

c. 1916 **22" long**

had a greater impact on the war than the mighty dreadnought warships because they got many men into the action fast.

Speaking of the dreadnoughts, though, these warships participated in one of the most dramatic battles of the war. The awesome fleets of Great Britain and Germany met only once, in the Battle of Jutland in the North Sea. Some fifty-eight dreadnoughts and many smaller vessels were engaged. While the outcome was inconclusive, Germany's declaration of victory seemed dubious because her ships never again sailed forth to challenge the British navy.

THE SHIP BUILDERS AND TOY MAKERS COMPETE

After the war, the great liners were spruced up and returned to passenger service. Great Britain, Germany, France, and Italy all competed for the business and tried especially to cater to the growing legion of American tourists. These countries not only competed for passengers, but for the prestige associated with the annual

blue ribbon award for the fastest liner. The British *Mauretania* held this distinction for twenty-two years. But it was soon bested by Germany's *Bremen* and *Europa*, Italy's *Rex*, France's *Normandie*, and then Britain's *Queen Mary*. The great ship builders were responding to a world enamored with speed. And the toy boat makers crafted vessels based on these famed liners, including many that made their way into the Forbes collection.

Incidentally, majestic ocean liners, military vessels, and riverboats (the oldest toy boats in the Forbes collection) weren't the only vessels that inspired the legendary toy makers of yesteryear. They also found that there was a market for whimsical designs, some of which were acquired by the Forbes family for its collection.

For example, there is an American-made Zippee speed-boat powered by a balloon attached to a tube emerging from the boat's stern. There is also the tin *L'Amphibo* boat-on-wheels. Rich in diversity and artistry, the "Ships Ahoy!" collection showcases the creativity and unsurpassed workmanship of the captains of the old-world toy boat industry.

MÄRKLIN GUNBOAT NEW YORK

Crafted in 1904, this painted tin gunboat is complete with its four-wheeled carriage. The rich details on the deck include twin funnels and masts, six cannons, a winch, four-bladed propeller, and a six-pointed ship's wheel controlling the rudder. The hull is olive green, black, and red, and the toy is stamped in red: Made in Germany. **22" long**

Märklin Battleship NEW YORK

25" long

Radiguet

31" long

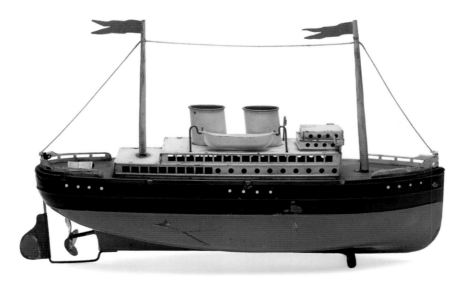

Fleischmann COLUMBUS

17½" long

CHAPTER 4

THE GREAT TOY BOAT COMPANIES AROSE TOGETHER IN NUREMBERG

"THE BEST OF OUR FLEET COME FROM TOY BOATS'
GOLDEN AGE—AROUND 1870 TO 1955. THIS WAS THE PERIOD
DURING WHICH THE MOST BEAUTIFUL AND MAGICAL OF
THESE VERY SPECIAL TIN PLAYTHINGS WERE MANUFACTURED
BY FIRMS WITH NAMES LIKE MÄRKLIN, BING, CARETTE..."

—Malcolm Forbes

Malcolm Forbes also cherished and collected toy boats made by the firms of Arnold, Falk, and Fleisch-mann which, like Märklin, Bing, and Carette, were located in Nuremberg, Germany. He and Robert Forbes were also impressed by the works of Maltête & Parent, Radiguet, and JEP of France; and Ives, Orkin, Brown, and James Fallows & Co. in this country ("My Fantasy Fleet," 1989).

In fact, while the Forbeses acknowledged Märklin as the industry leader and Bing and Fleischmann as viable competitors, they felt the leaders' toys were often equaled by Falk, Carette, Arnold, and Radiguet. One thing that most of these companies had in common is that most of the toy boats they made were based on highly visible ships of the period. They were usually powered with steam engines, battery-powered motors, or clockwork motors.

Another common thread among these firms is that

ous, a 20-minute clockwork motor. Märklin was the only company to sell sailors with their toy boats. The company is still in existence today.

Bing

The other highly prominent Nuremberg toy maker—and a legitimate competitor to Märklin—was Gebrüder Bing. Founded by Ignatius and Adolph Bing, the company enjoyed fame for its spring-driven toys. Bing made everything from ocean liners to motorboats, and Bing toys were distinguished by superb workmanship and detail, yet they typically cost less than comparable Märklin toys. But Bing offered less ornamentation and coloration than Märklin.

"Bing produced three series each of ocean liners and warships, various submarines and other boats as well," notes Robert Forbes. While very few toy boats remain from the company's first series—which was produced between 1890

THE GLAMOUR OF OCEAN LINERS GAVE WAY
TO A FASCINATION WITH AIRPLANES, WHICH CAUSED
THE TOY COMPANIES TO PHASE OUT TOY BOATS

many of them sprang up at about the same time: Märklin in 1859, Bing in 1865, Plank in 1866, Ives in 1868, Schoenner in 1875, Carette in 1886, Fleischmann in 1887, and Falk in the late 1890s.

Together, they created the Golden Era of Toy Boats.

Märklin

The industry's undisputed leader, the Märklin Company, crafted marvelous toy boats and enriched them with such details as removable lifeboats, steering bridges, lead anchors, and hand-painted crewmen. Märklin toy boats were—and still are—the most prestigious and the most sought after of all. Märklin produced three series of ocean liners, three of warships, and a group of submarines. The company also offered three different propulsion systems: a six-hour electric motor, a one-hour steam engine, and, by far the most numer-

and 1910—the Forbes collection includes some particularly important restored boats from subsequent series.

"Bing's first series of ocean liners [1890–1901] was comparable to the most beautiful Märklins of the time," says Robert Forbes. "In Bing's second series of ocean liners [1910–1914], electric motors were introduced, but the series itself was generally less sophisticated than the Märklin counterparts. In the third series [1914–1928] are, perhaps, some of the most pleasant toy boats ever made. They are often large—up to one meter long—but the lines are well proportioned to their size and evoke that delicious sense of grand illusion in miniature.

"The first Bing warships appeared in catalogues around 1898, and are as rare and valuable today as the first series from Märklin. However, their quality began to fall off before the First World War, most noticeably in the detailing.

BING OCEAN LINER **BREMEN**

Like many toy ocean liners, this one is inspired by a famous ship—in this case the German *Bremen*. Originally built in France and dubbed the *Pasteur* in 1939, it was used to transport troops during and after World War II. In 1957, the ship was purchased by North German Lloyd and became the ocean liner *Bremen*, providing exemplary passenger service until 1959. Several owners—including Chandris Cruise Lines—subsequently sailed this ship, which operated under various names. According to at least one historical account, when the ship was called the *Filipinas Saudi I*, it sank in the Indian Ocean on June 9, 1980. The original ship was nearly 700 feet long. Like the original, the toy is crafted with three red, white, and black stacks, and the stairways go from the top deck to the sun deck to the main deck. **26" long**

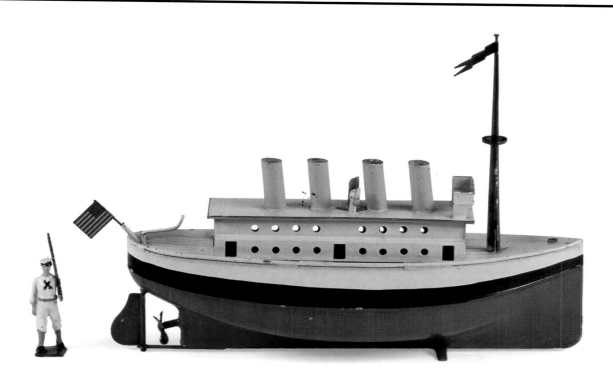

BING PASSENGER LINER

This impressive wind-up toy is crowned with four tall stacks and raised deck. c. 1920 **15" long**

THE MÄRKLIN LEGACY

When tinsmith Theodor Friedrich Wilhelm Märklin (1817–1866) decided to start making doll house accessories in 1859—particularly tinplate kitchenware—he had no idea what lay in store for him and his fledgling enterprise. The Märklin Company would go on to become one of the great toy manufacturers of all time, producing cars, boats, and other fascinating playthings fashioned of tin.

Aiding Theodor in the business was his second wife, Caroline (1826–1893), whom he married in the royal Württemberg borough of Göppingen, where he had lived since 1840. Caroline, who espoused views held by political economist Friedrich List, brought enormous enthusiasm and a sharp intellect to the business. Within a few years, Theodor and Caroline had created considerable demand for their products and were able to move into larger living and working accommodations.

Unfortunately, Theodor would meet his untimely demise in an accident in 1866, an event that threatened to derail the company's progress. But Caroline showed her true mettle, managing the company through some difficult times for twenty years. She was hoping that her sons would take over, but alas, they showed no interest in the toy business. Caroline remarried in 1868 and it wasn't until after her second husband passed away that one of her sons, Eugen Märklin (1861–1947), decided that he was, in fact, at least somewhat interested in the Märklin business. Eugen continued to work a full-time job while giving part-time attention to the toy company.

Märklin's Success Was a Family Affair

Eugen and his brother Karl must have come to the conclusion that the Märklin business had real potential. Together, they formed an unlimited trading company in 1888 and incorporated the family toy company. The firm was then known as Gebrüder Märklin (also spelled Mäerklin). Although the business struggled for a number of years afterward, Eugen Märklin must have inherited his parents' determination, optimism, and vision for the future. And, like his father, Eugen was blessed with a wife who helped and encouraged her husband to persevere in the business.

MÄRKLIN JUPITER
Eight hand-painted figures sit on two benches on the deck. Note also the anchor and lifeboat. **27" long**

MÄRKLIN **BREMEN** OCEANLINER

Here's a curious hybrid of a passenger liner, armed with deck guns, which was common during World War I. This unusual toy is the gift of Charles Sweet, who received it new as a boy. c. 1915 **23" long**

MÄRKLIN BATTLESHIP **NEW YORK**

This clockwork boat exemplifies the finest of the toy maker's art, with its charming exaggerations emphasizing the "toy-ness" of the boat while still maintaining a standard of excellence in the hand-painted details. Among its fascinating details are numerous cannons and a lifeboat. c. 1900 **41" long**

In 1891, Eugen Märklin made a major business decision that would ultimately determine the success or failure of Gebrüder Märklin. He decided to take over the Ludwig Lutz tinplate toy factory in Ellwangen. While this company's products had been very popular in Germany and elsewhere for decades, Lutz's tradition of crafting handmade products proved too costly for the company to compete effectively. Eugen Märklin invited Lutz's employees to come to work in Göppingen for Gebrüder Märklin.

Eugen had the keen business sense to recognize that the Lutz Company had experience and skills that would prove beneficial to Gebrüder Märklin. With the Lutz people onboard, Eugen Märklin was able to strike a balance between inexpensive and mechanical methods of mass production on the one hand, and lithographic printing and costly hand workmanship on the other.

Under the stewardship of Eugen and Karl, Gebrüder Märklin went well beyond the original product line of doll house accessories. They produced enameled tinplate boats, carousels, and aeronautical toys. Gebrüder Märklin quickly became the leader in manufacturing clockwork, steam, and electric toy trains. And it was Gebrüder Märklin that first introduced standardized tinplate tracks in 1891.

Märklin Experiments with Toy Boats

Among its many product lines, Gebrüder Märklin truly excelled at making highly detailed toy boats. They unveiled their first series of ocean liners around the turn of the century. As Robert Forbes has noted, these ocean liners weren't meant to be exact scale reproductions or precise replicas. Instead, they derived their charm from their delightful exaggerations of particular features. The second series, inspired by the great ocean liners of the period, came out in the '20s and '30s. These were the grand years of ocean travel, and the Gebrüder Märklin toy ships captured the spirit and glamour of those days. For the third Gebrüder Märklin series (1930–1936), ocean liners were eclipsed by warships as Germany prepared itself for war.

While warships weren't initially very popular—and few were made by Gebrüder Märklin until 1906—the firm began developing military vessels at an unprecedented rate. The company came out with a very impressive squadron of battleships, cruisers, and torpedo boats. Subsequently, Gebrüder Märklin's third series (1918–1936) became more bland, favoring realism over delightful exaggeration. Most of these toy boats were based on the *Linienschiffe*—or ships of the line—modeled on the lines of the great battleships of that tumultuous era.

Just as the Märklin firm created the finest toy ocean liners and battleships, they also set the benchmark for toy submarines. By this time, they had perfected the clockwork mechanism, which enabled the toy submarines to dive and return to the surface repeatedly until the clockwork ran out, at which point the submarine resurfaced and could be rewound for another mission.

Gebrüder Märklin continued to produce the finest toys, many of which are now rare, valuable, and highly sought after. However, as tin toy boat manufacturing came to an end in the 1950s—in part, at least, because the new plastic toys were so much cheaper—Gebrüder Märklin made the move necessary for survival: it began making plastic train sets.

Nevertheless, the Märklin toy boat legacy lives on. Some of the company's very best—and most desirable—antique boats can be seen in the Forbes Galleries "Ships Ahoy!" collection, as well as in the pages of this book.

"Bing submarines were more modest than Märklin's but nonetheless had a great allure. Their charm stemmed from the fact that they were toys of special fantasy, resembling nothing as much as the *Nautilus* of Jules Verne."

Among Märklin's and Bing's best works were their riverboats. Unlike the imposing ocean liners and warships, they were gentle in appearance and spirit, evoking the pleasure of a cruise down a tranquil waterway on a warm, summer evening.

Fleischmann

Among the other legendary Nuremberg toy boat makers was the Fleischmann firm, which is still in existence. Fleischmann began producing toy ocean liners at the turn of the century, ceased production during World War I, then resumed making toy boats until 1958, except during World War II. In addition to ocean liners, Fleischmann and Company produced battleships, warships, and flying boats. Today the company is known for its superb model railroads.

FLEISCHMANN AIRCRAFT CARRIER

Fleischmann made toy warships all the way up to 1955. This particular toy is a rare example of the warship that developed in part because of the influence of General Billy Mitchell, a man decidedly ahead of his time. As head of aviation in the Army Signal Corps during World War I, he foresaw the day when air power would be decisive in war. Throughout his career he battled his superiors, who felt that the airplane wasn't good for much more than observation. Finally, he persuaded the Army and the Navy to see if planes could sink captured German warships. The *Ostfriesland* was quickly sent to the bottom of the Atlantic Ocean, infuriating Mitchell's superiors. Apparently they were too stubborn to realize that by proving that a big warship could be destroyed from the air, Mitchell had personally precipitated a whole new era in naval warfare. Although he was court-martialed in 1925, Mitchell's confidence in air power was validated in World War II, the first war in which air superiority proved decisive. Mitchell was posthumously awarded a special Congressional medal in 1946. And his legacy lives on in a Fleischmann warship crafted with a full complement of gun turrets. **14" long**

CARETTE BATTLESHIP

Made in France in 1908, this is a rare and important antique toy battleship. The many deck details include two anchors, a working winch, deck rails, companionways, main and secondary armament, a raised bridge with fire direction control, searchlights, two lifeboats and davits, ventilators, and an engine room skylight. The zinc hull is fitted with a key-wound clockwork motor. The owner of this toy battleship could remove the superstructure to reveal the mechanism. **26" long**

ARNOLD U29 1941 GERMAN SUBMARINE

During World War II, the German U-boats inflicted heavy damage on the Allied forces, including the sinking of the British aircraft carrier *HMS Courageous* off the Irish coast. In this toy sub, Arnold depicts a U29 submarine. Decorated with a swastika and eagle on the conning tower, crafted with a camouflage top, and painted with a blue and red hull, it looks almost as menacing as a toy as it did as a full-size submarine. **13" long**

Carette

Also working in Nuremberg was George Carette, a French photographer. Although he was a French nationalist, he moved to Germany and worked with Bing before founding his own firm in partnership with Paul Josefsthal. At the Universal Exhibition of 1893, Carette presented the first electric train. Many of Carette's toys were sold in England through Basset-Lowke stores. The Forbes collection features Carette boats, including those with a wind-up key protruding from a smokestack. In 1917, the Germans deported Carette and closed his firm.

Falk & Schoenner

Just as Carette left Bing and became a rival, a Carette employee—Joseph Falk—left Carette and started his own company. Falk specialized in steam-driven toys and magic lanterns. He used Schoenner plans and casting molds when Schoenner's firm folded in 1913. Jean Schoenner had started his German firm in 1875, and while his toys were of very high quality, they weren't as detailed as the more successful competitors. Likewise, Falk's toy boats weren't as good as those made by Bing and Märklin, and their funnels were disproportionately short compared with the other manufacturers. The J. Falk company was taken over in 1925 by Ernest Plank, makers of tin trains, airplanes, automobiles, and, of course, boats.

JEP

Founded in 1899 in Paris, the firm of Jouet became JEP in 1929, after the merger of SIF and JdeP (Jouets de Paris). Jouet produced highly complex toy cars and boats. In 1965, the factory closed.

Arnold

While many of the manufacturers of wind-up boats placed the keys in the stacks, Karl Arnold often had them emerge from the boat's stern. Karl Arnold started producing toy boats in Nuremberg, Germany, in 1906. The First World War interrupted production, and sadly, the company's archives for the early years were destroyed between World War I and II. What we do know is that the firm produced many ocean liners, and after 1945, they made some boats and submarines. Around 1950 Arnold stopped making toy boats altogether and focused solely on model trains.

Ives

While the German companies dominated the toy boat business, American and French companies also produced boats of beauty and detail. For example, the U.S. firm Ives, founded in 1868 by Edward R. Ives in Plymouth, Connecticut, developed clockwork-driven toy ocean liners with the slogan "Ives Toys Make Happy Boys."

The company moved to Bridgeport, Connecticut, in 1870, and by the 1880s, they were leaders in superb clockwork toys designed by Jerome Secor, Nathan Warner, and Arthur Hotchkiss. Known for toy electric trains, Ives also produced destroyers, tugboats, and ocean liners between 1917 and 1928. Because intricate detailing increases the already high cost of tooling, the Ives boats lacked much of the realism that distinguished the European counterparts. Ives failed financially with toy boats, and the ones they made haven't held up against the test of time because their paint peeled off quickly. (They weren't painted with a primer.) The firm filed for bankruptcy in 1929, another victim of the Depression, and Lionel took over.

Bliss

Among Ives's fellow American toy boat makers was the R. Bliss Manufacturing Company of Pawtucket, Rhode Island. Founded by Rufus Bliss, this company made toys for a full century. Bliss was a pioneer in the development of lithographed paper on wooden toys, including boats. The company was eventually sold to Mason & Parker of Winchendon, Massachusetts.

KW

While not nearly so well known as the other Nuremberg toy makers—and represented by only one toy boat in this book—KW was founded in 1895 by Wilhelm Krauss and the firm shut down in 1938.

Weeden

Another toy company that cropped up in New England was the Weeden Manufacturing Company of New Bedford, Massachusetts, founded by William N. Weeden. Known for producing a working toy steam engine in 1884, the company made toy steamboats and steam-driven fire engines and automobiles. Weeden also made clockwork tin mechanical banks, including *Ding Dong Bell* and *Japanese Ball Tosser*, both of which are collectibles.

Orkin

One of the most interesting American toy boat makers was Samuel Orkin. Like the Forbes family, he acted on more than money. He felt that it was his mission in life to make military vessels that would inspire American boys to become war heroes. Perhaps his greatest achievement was a "toy" inspired by the dreadnought *Arkansas*. It was nine feet long and drew more than eight ounces of water. Powered by seven electric motors, it was said to achieve a speed exceeding four knots. The current was generated by an eight-volt storage battery designed to provide consistent output.

The boat was equipped with a double bottom containing eighteen compartments, including bulkheads filled with compressed air and smoke. When the toy was displayed, naval experts were awestruck when the four three-ounce anchors were hoisted and the boat traveled across a miniature lake. Imagine their surprise when the guns fired for nearly three minutes. Tiny soldiers paced the upper and lower decks, saluting officers as they passed by.

Radiguet

In addition to the German and American toy makers represented in the Forbes Collection, there is also a French company founded by Radiguet in Paris around 1850. The firm became known as Radiguet & Fils and produced mostly boats and trains. Powered by steam and sporting wooden decks, Radiguet boats of the 1880s and 1890s often had striking belle époque features such as elegant figureheads and delicate fo'c'sle grillwork. Members of the firm won their first award, a silver medal, at the Universal Exposition of 1878.

The next year, they won a gold medal. Just after 1900, Radiguet merged with Massiot, and the firm became Radiguet & Massiot. This firm was noteworthy for toy boats with machinery above the decks—such as a brass boiler, steam valves, and moving parts crafted of steel. This kind of prominent detail gave these French toys an air of elegance.

The Japanese

Very few toy boats were made right up to World War II. However, after the Second World War, some companies began making toy boats again. Joining the surviving toy companies were Japanese firms that began making toy boats to aid in the postwar recovery. Soon they dominated the industry with painted and lithographed tin toys that were both highly unusual and less expensive than those made by the traditional German manufacturers.

THE END OF AN ERA

The ultimate decline of the manufacture of the great toy boats can be traced to two principal causes. Robert Forbes says, "The two world wars, of course, took their toll on German toy production, but it was the introduction of plastic that changed the toy world forever; the phasing out of ocean liners in favor of the airplane also helped bring about a halt to the manufacturing of toy boats."[3]

In his *Spirit of St. Louis*, Charles Lindbergh made the first solo flight across the Atlantic in 1927, giving the world a glimpse into the future of long-range flight. Then, a dozen years later, the Pan American Clipper *Dixie* flew from Long Island Sound to Portugal. This ushered in an entirely new sign of progress: scheduled transatlantic service by air. The glamour of ocean liners gave way to a fascination with airplanes, which caused the toy companies to phase out toy boats by the mid '50s.

So the surviving legends of toy boat-making focused on other products—including toy trains and, of course, planes. And since no one has crafted big, intricate toy boats for so long, they have had plenty of time to become more rare, more prized, and more valuable.

WEEDEN LIVE STEAMSHIP

This steam-powered vessel, made in the U.S., is stamped *Weeden* on the deck. **14½" long**

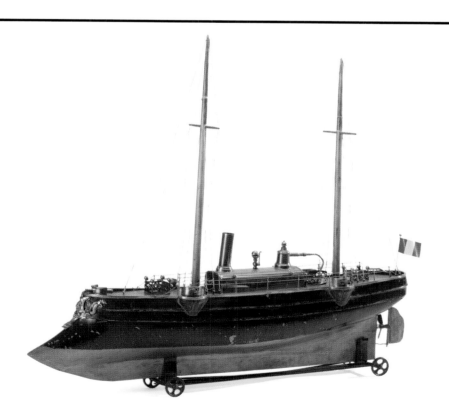

RADIGUET & MASSIOT WARSHIP

Radiguet & Massiot was known for crafting toy boats with shiny machinery above the decks, particularly brass. This stunning vessel is a perfect example, and its small brass cannons actually fired. **31" long**

BING PUMPER

c. 1925 8½" long

BING BLUE & WHITE SUBMARINE

8½" long

CARETTE MERCHANT MARINE

c. 1902 19" long

CHAPTER 5

WHAT MAKES THESE BOATS SO RARE AND VALUABLE?

"IF ANYONE SHOULD SEEK MY ADVICE ABOUT
COLLECTING, I'D QUICKLY POINT OUT THE OLD TRUTH—
BUY ONLY WHAT YOU LIKE. MEASURE A WORK BY
THE JOY AND SATISFACTION IT WILL BRING."

—Malcolm Forbes

Antique toy boats, especially those of high quality, are rare, even more so than other old toys. There are several reasons for their rapid disappearance from our world. First, the best toys came out in lower volumes than other mass-produced toys because they were more expensive than most playthings.

But this doesn't fully explain why so few survived. Another reason for their rarity is exemplified by Malcolm Forbes's personal experience:

"Toy boats in the Forbes family were more prized than electric trains or other playthings," he once said. "We were forever sailing them in nearby brooks and streams and in summers on lakes and oceans. Not a one of them survived to be part of this collection. But the memory of them and the joy of them account for its formation."

When Malcolm Forbes says, "Not a one of them survived," he is typical of many a toy boat owner. In the foreword of the book *Toy Boats 1870–1955: A Pictorial History*,

When he was just a boy, Robert's toy boats became extinct for still another reason, which was no doubt common among other boys who had similar vessels. Robert recalls how he perfected methods of sinking and destroying his toys. "At one point I had about a dozen tin boats," he said, "but then I got a BB gun." You can just imagine what he did with that gun.

FEW ANTIQUE TOY BOATS SURVIVE TO THIS DAY

But little seamen weren't the only cause of drowned boats. Small sailboats were often laden with so much canvas that they capsized from the weight of rain. Clockwork motors often carried boats well beyond a child's reach and even beyond view. The hydrofoil technology used in early submarines wasn't terribly reliable, causing subs to descend to the floor of a pond or lake, never to rise again.

THE GRAND VESSELS THAT HAVE COURSED THROUGH THE WORLD'S GREAT WATERS STILL INSPIRE WONDER AND AWE

co-written by his son Robert, Malcolm Forbes poses and answers his own question:

"Why are old toy boats so relatively rare these days? Because they survive less than other toys for the very same reasons that real boats survive less long than most other manufactured things. Such toys were for playing with in the water. In the tub, recovering the sunk was easy, though resulting rust eventually took its toll. The most fun was sailing them on lakes and at seashores where recovery was more difficult and very frequently impossible. As with the real ones, the more toy boats did their thing, the less likely they were to survive."

Many a toy boat failed to survive high winds, fickle tides, the ravages of corrosion, and, of course, amateur seamanship. What's more, there's something about boats that brings out the daring, recklessness, and mischievous side of a boy. Take Robert Forbes, for example.

And some of the larger toy yachts were so difficult to navigate that one wonders if an experienced captain could have kept them afloat.

Last, but probably not least, was the way most toy boat manufacturers provided access to the engine room. You had to lift off the entire superstructure to get to the engine. Since the lids weren't exactly watertight, water could get inside while the toy boat was in the water. This factor contributed to the sinking of toy boats.

The good news is that the antique toy boats that did survive have attracted the interest of collectors in recent times, in no small part because of the Forbes family's collecting fervor. In today's collecting universe, surviving tinplate and cast-iron toys are expensive and hotly pursued by knowledgeable collectors. Reflecting this phenomenon, the investment firm of Merrill Lynch ran an ad in 1991 that carried the follow-

B I N G S H I P S

(top) Submarine and Ship; (bottom) Lighthouse and Ships

HOW MUCH
DID THE ORIGINALS COST?

In the Forbes Galleries there are toy boats that originally sold for less than a dollar, including a 1910 Bing speedboat that sold for 79¢ in 1912 by Sears, Roebuck & Co. There are also toys that cost over $50. And, if a toy cost that much around the turn of the century, imagine what the equivalent cost would be today!

Because the price range for toy boats was so extreme, these toys on the whole were very popular. However, the better ones—including many now preserved in the Forbes Galleries—were only purchased by the affluent.

Take Märklin, for example. The toy boats shown in an early twentieth century catalog could be had for as little as $1.50 (still a lot of money in those days) for a small clockwork-driven steamer, or as much as $54 for a battleship nearly four feet long. What would you get for so much money? Well, this particular battleship featured a steam engine, brass boiler, fixed-cylinder engine, alcohol burner, safety valve, moveable gun turrets, mortars, and guns that fired.

Just like the full-size ship, this so-called toy was equipped with ship's boats, moveable davits, companionways, decks, turret masts, searchlights, flags, and a semaphore. But that's not all. The crew on board numbered some forty figures crafted of lead. And, while the boat could run for more than an hour, you could pay a few dollars more for a very desirable option: a battery-powered electric motor that would extend the running time to six full hours!

Pricey Toys Become Priceless Collectibles

In between the low-end and high-end extremes were some very nice toys at mid-range prices. And many of these more moderate toy boats can also be found in the Forbes collection. In the same Märklin catalog that promoted the $1.50 and $54 toys, there was a frigate measuring more than two feet in length for $15 and a richly detailed ocean liner for $34.

In 1910, most toys could be had for pennies. Coca-Cola® was 5¢ a glass. You could get a Kodak camera for as little as $5 and a nice suit for $50. In 1914, Ford Motor Company was considered a generous employer when it announced that it would pay its workers $5 a day. In this context, paying $15, $35, or $50 for a toy boat would be quite an extravagance. So, in relative terms, the better toy boats were expensive.

But they were worth every penny!

WALBERT THE SINKING BATTLESHIP WITH TORPEDO

Made by Walbert Manufactuing Company, *The Sinking Battleship* came in two parts, hinged in the middle. A button held the parts together. When the toy torpedo—wound with a rubber band—hit the button, the ship broke apart and sank. **13½" long**

ing tagline: "If you ever doubted the value of a long-term investment philosophy, go back to your childhood." The concept behind the ad is that if you had held on to certain childhood possessions, you might get a windfall if you sold them today. Among the treasures shown in the ad was a 1905 gunboat from the Forbes collection.

HOW MUCH IS AN ANTIQUE TOY BOAT WORTH?

So let's say you come across a vintage toy boat in your attic in nearly pristine condition. What might it be worth? It depends on how rare the toy is and how badly some collector wants it. But suffice it to say that these toys are worth a lot more than they used to be, again mainly because the Forbeses redefined their worth by breaking records for amounts paid for toy boats at auctions.

"Most of the spending records we break are our own," Malcolm Forbes said in "My Fantasy Fleet." "And for a Scotsman it's not a comforting thought to be breaking auction records. But when something turns us on, we go after it. There's solace, though, in setting records sometimes. For instance, we had almost 300 toy boats when the German battleship *Weissenberg*, made by the master toysmiths at Märklin, came up, and the keen competition for it led us to pay a spectacular toy-price record—$21,000. It was a lot to spend for a tin boat, but there was bound to be substantial rub-off value on the other 299 boats in the collection. In the end, though, you can only measure a work by the joy and satisfaction it will bring. If you want to collect as an investment, become a dealer."

According to Dana Hawkes, an antiques expert who worked at Sotheby's for years, it is for toys that are in mint condition, and that have not been restored, that people pay a premium. Any kind of restoration, no matter how expertly done, will cause the value of a collectible toy to depreciate, she explains; and the gallery or auction house selling the antique should be more than happy to provide the potential buyer with a condition report noting any restoration in its description of the toy.

Collectible toy boats are generally more than fifty to one hundred years old. That's because manufacturers stopped making them in the '50s, and toy watercraft have never been produced the way they once were—as veritable masterworks of the toy maker's craft.

KIDS TURN THEIR EYES TO THE SKIES

But why did their appeal diminish in the '50s? Not long after World War II, the world's great ships were eclipsed by commercial airliners as the preferred mode of traveling long distances. Instead of gazing at rivers and oceans and imagining watery adventures, children began looking to the skies and playing with craft that could defy gravity and soar among the clouds, or planets. As the technology of aviation continued to advance, children could play with the craft that took astronauts into outer space and with the vehicles of fantasy and cinema. How could a child entranced with the likes of *Star Wars* and *Apollo 13* be expected to appreciate the lore of the riverboat?

Yet, when one observes the children who come to the Forbes Galleries, it is obvious that the grand vessels that have coursed through the world's great waters still inspire wonder and awe. While they may never again interest toy makers in making truly magnificent toys, one can visit the Forbes Galleries to rekindle the spirit of innovation and adventure that must have driven the great ship makers and toy builders of the past to create vessels of enduring beauty, meaning, and romance.

THE MORE TOY BOATS DID THEIR THING, THE LESS LIKELY THEY WERE TO SURVIVE

OUR SAILOR BOY BLOCKS

Within the fascinating "Ships Ahoy!" collection is a small room created to depict the **Land of Counterpane**, inspired by a poem written by Robert Louis Stevenson. Inside the tiny room are many items—including this toy boat manufactured by the Bliss Company of Rhode Island. It's actually a puzzle with block edges that show sailors. **9½" x 12¾"**

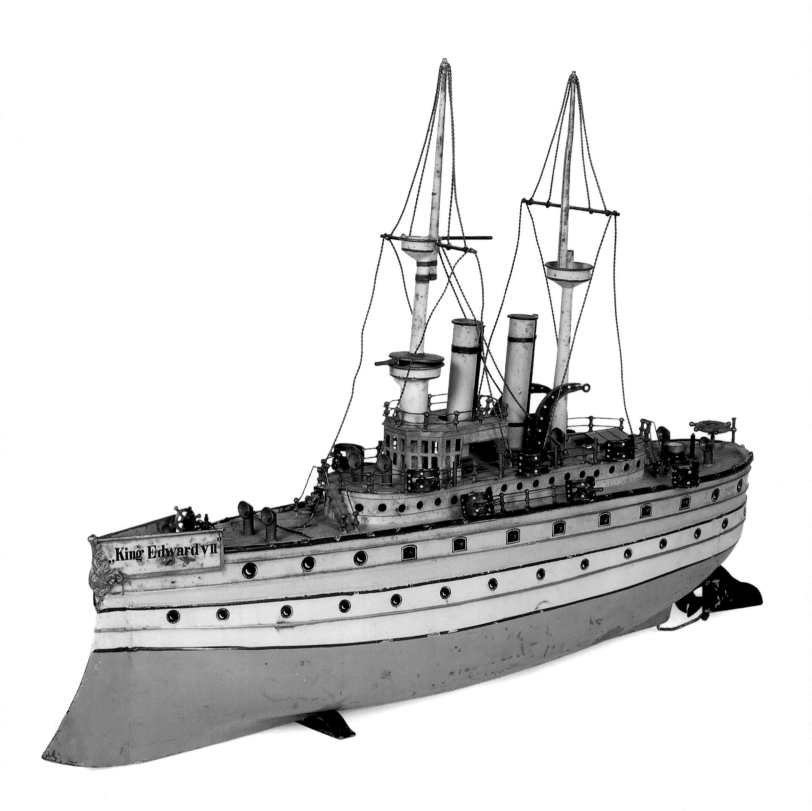

PLANK KING EDWARD VII

On January 6, 1916, a British King Edward VII class battleship hit a mine laid by the Germans. The explosion under the starboard engine room caused the ship to list. Attempts to tow her failed, and after about five hours, the ship was abandoned and sank. Despite the occasional calamity, King Edward VII class battleships were among the finest and most impressive of their time, inspiring many German toy makers, including Plank, to create powerful looking toy boats. This well-armed ship has two smokestacks and a pair of masts with intricate rigging. **29" long**

CHAPTER 6

MEET SOME OF THE BRIGHTEST STARS IN THE COLLECTION

"BOATS AND THE SEA ALWAYS HAD STRONG APPEAL FOR ME."

—Malcolm Forbes

While many toys have attracted collectors and commanded lofty prices over the years, in many ways the toy boat is in a category all its own. Unlike baseball cards, stamps, coins, or die-cast cars, toy boats are often elaborate creations, mimicking in so many ways the myriad details and accessories found on the original vessels. And, unlike a train that can always use a new car or a doll that can be dressed up with new outfits, a toy boat needs no further enhancements or additions.

Way back when kids bought and played with these boats, they could imagine themselves captains conquering the roughest seas, fighting explosive naval battles, or negotiating tricky currents in big, wide rivers. And every time one of the finest toy boats sank or rusted away in someone's attic, the world lost a little of its magic. For these were no ordinary toys. They were mechanical marvels, the products of highly skilled craftsmen who paid considerable attention to every exquisite nuance, right down to the hand-painted details. The "Ships Ahoy!" collection is a testament to the companies and individuals who elevated the toy to a work of art.

"Our guideline for the collection was simply to make it as comprehensive as possible," Robert Forbes said in "Capitalist Toys," "with representation of all possible manufacturers in as many sizes as we could get. Unlike most collectors, however, for us condition was far less important. We figured that while a few mint pieces were desirable, it was more appropriate that the toys had fulfilled some of their life's purpose, which was to be played with. Also, for us, restored toys represented an inexpensive opportunity to complete a maker's fleet. And besides, when the boats ended up on display both in our touring show and in the Galleries, 99.9% of the visitors didn't care at all."

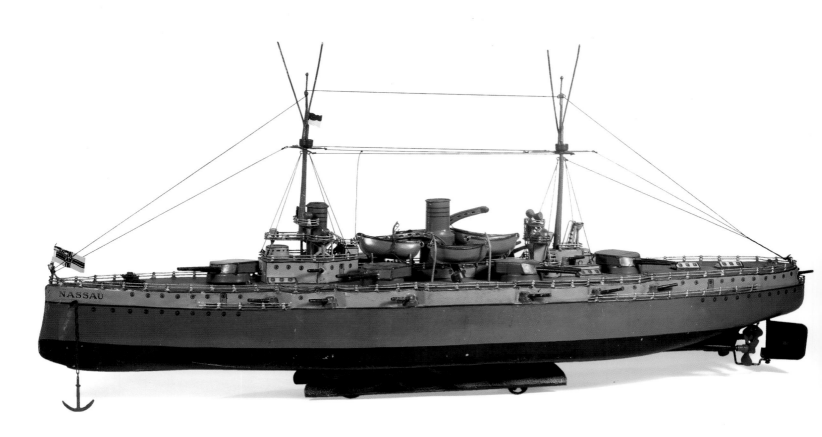

MÄRKLIN BATTLESHIP NASSAU

Acquired for $26,500 in 1988 at Sotheby's, London, this is one of the most important antique toy boats in the Forbes Galleries. The richly varied array of deck details include six revolving guns, a bridge, searchlights, twin funnels, two derricks, two lifeboats on davits, and an anchor. Hand-painted in three-tone gray with simulated planked hull, this toy battleship was propelled by a clockwork mechanism driving the three screws at the stern.
35½" long

THE FORBES BIG BOATS
BECAME TOY BOATS

Given the Forbes family tradition of ocean voyages and collecting toy boats, it's no surprise that they also enjoyed collecting full-size vessels. After all, *Forbes* magazine is an important enterprise, and many companies own their own transportation vehicles, even if they are usually planes. In any case, the Forbeses had five corporate yachts in all. And all five can be inspected in the form of intricate scale models within the Forbes Galleries.

The first corporate Forbes boat was a 72-foot *Highlander* acquired in 1955. It was a converted Canadian boat, and the original vessel served the Dominion Navy during World War II, so this *Highlander* had quite a history.

A few months after buying their first boat, the Forbeses commissioned the Dutch shipbuilding consortium, Feadship, to build a 98-foot steel yacht to be designed by Fritz de Voogt. This second *Highlander* was launched in 1957, and it proved to be quite an asset to *Forbes* magazine, providing a lovely setting for entertaining corporate executives during the next decade. And, now that the Forbeses knew that these luxurious boats were proving to be sound investments, they decided that a larger one was needed.

So a new and more impressive *Highlander* was on the drafting tables by 1964, and construction was complete in March 1967 at Adlsmeer, Netherlands. The spanking new *Highlander* arrived in New York in June of that year with the entire Forbes family aboard, fresh from a voyage that had begun in Istanbul six weeks earlier. The career of this third *Highlander* ended when it was consumed by an accidental blaze, inspiring an editorial in *Fact and Comment* entitled "A Death in the Family."

Forbes's **Highlanders** *Are Good for Business*

Before the third *Highlander* was reduced to ashes in 1980, she had made quite an impression on well-heeled men and women, including Forbes business associates and dignitaries and heads of state. Kings, prime ministers, and presidents—both American and foreign—were entertained aboard this spacious yacht. Major American corporate mergers resulted from friendships formed on the *Highlander*. And the Forbeses have intimated that more publicity arose from conversations aboard the *Highlander* than from any ship since Noah's ark and Christopher Columbus's wee fleet.

The fourth *Highlander* was built by the same firm and designed by the same marine architect as her two predecessors. She, too, served admirably in the same elegant Forbes tradition. Then it took over three years to transform the fifth *Highlander* from vision to a yacht distinguished by the fruits of the soaring imagination and genius of her designer, Jon Bannenberg.

Launched in November of 1985, the ship is over 150 feet long, 29 feet 3 inches of the beam, with a draft of 9 feet 9 inches. Its displacement is 477 tons. Capable of worldwide sailing, the fifth Forbes *Highlander* is powered by twin G.M. 16V149 diesels that deliver 1,800 horsepower, providing an average cruising speed of 13.7 knots with a top speed of 14.3 knots. Electric power comes from 140-kilowatt G.M. generators. The ship has a water capacity of 5,300 gallons and fuel capacity of 19,700 gallons, providing the latest *Highlander* with a cruising range of over 4,000 nautical miles.

The ship has five guest staterooms, six salons, six staterooms for the crew, and 14 heads. On board are a Bell Jet Ranger III helicopter, two tenders (a 19-foot Cigarette and a 23-foot Danzi), and two Harley-Davidson 1,340 cc, 5-speed motorcycles. The *Highlander* has a crew of 14, including the captain. And, when it was completed, the Forbeses were confident that this extraordinary ship had set the direction, style, and high standard of quality for yachts to try to emulate for many years to come.

NOAH'S ARK

Made in 1910, this imaginative boat is lithographed in many colors on the sides, front, and back, and hand painted on the roof and hull. Noah and his entourage appear on front, and birds grace the back. The various wildlife that came two by two are visible on the sides. **11" long**

AN INTERVIEW
WITH ROBERT L. FORBES

Q. When the toys were originally purchased, were they considered the province of the well-to-do? Were some types within the reach of the average person? How pricey were the best ones relative to other tin toys most people might buy?

A. In the collection, there are boats of many sizes made from many types of material that reflect a full array of prices paid at the time of their manufacture. The larger boats were very expensive at the time, and the detailing along with the means of propulsion—clockwork, steam, or battery—would affect the price as well. I imagine that the biggest boats in the collection were certainly intended for the very well off, and most likely bought for children but played with mostly by the dad! Never inexpensive for the era, the tin boats of smaller size came out in much larger numbers, and some of the wooden toys with glued-on lithographed paper would have been very affordable. The biggest and finest of the boats would have carried price tags equivalent to a very large train set.

Q. You and your father pretty much established a new price benchmark for rare, antique toy boats. Do you have a feel for whether your acquisitions have risen or fallen in value, especially the most expensive ones like the *Weissenberg* and *Lusitania?*

A. Though we collected at a time when boats were rarely seen, we did have to pay top dollar to get the top pieces, setting a few records on the way. But bear in mind too that though we ended up paying the highest price, there was someone else willing to pay a bit less for it as well. I'm sure now that at auction, these pieces would do far better than what we paid for them, as evidenced by what dealers are charging today for equivalent pieces. Crown jewels like the *Weissenberg* or the *Lusitania* would certainly fetch top dollar were examples like them to be found.

Q. What is the current climate for rare toy boats in terms of prices and availability?

A. I still look at the auction houses' toy catalogues and rarely see great boats come up anymore, so I think that the market is strong for fine pieces, as it is in the art market these days; getting good material is harder than ever.

Q. What impact do you think the Forbes collection of toy boats has had on the visibility, importance, and desirability of toy boats among collectors?

A. No question, the visibility of the Forbes collection brought about a great focus in the antique toy world on toy boats. Up to that time there had been a few collectors, but infinitely more for toy cars, trains, and dolls. Because the boats were rare to start with, the appearance of a major collector willing to spend what was necessary to obtain fine pieces caused a lot of boats to appear on the market over a period of years, but never all that many. It made other toy collectors rethink what they had and started a few on the toy boat road as well.

Q. Margaret Trombly [Vice President of the Forbes collections] says you have original packaging for some of the boats. How does the existence of the packaging affect the value? Can you estimate how much your models are worth with the packaging vs. how much less they would be worth without it?

A. Original packaging certainly adds to a boat because it is part of the boat's origins; it is how it was sent to the market, and it is how it was likely received by some youngster. Often there would be a lyrical, nautical scene on the package, making for great period visuals, but the more dramatic packaging usually meant a smaller boat inside. The great big boats normally came in a plain wooden crate, needing little heralding for the treasure inside. I would say an original package can add 15% to 30% more to the boat's value. Remember, too, that if the toy is in its original box, in all likelihood it will be in very good to pristine condition as well.

Q. What are your favorites in the collection and why?

A. I have too many favorites to list, but here are a few: *L'Amphibo* I enjoy for its belle époque splendor and whimsy. The Märklin ocean liners *Spree* and *Mauretania*, because their lines are so pretty and evoke the glamour of ocean travel; the large Märklin second series warship the *Posen* is a Great White Fleet dreadnought that encapsulates the history that led up to the Battle of Jutland in the First World War; Schoenner's *Aviso Greif* also sits pretty in the water and still has enough original paint to let you see that it must have been a splendid toy. The tin lithographed boat on page 42 that was probably made to celebrate the Japanese victory over the Russians in 1904 is a splendid floor toy I never tire of; and even the cast metal bank of the *Oregon* charms me with its exaggerated guns and lifeboats that are intended to fire young imaginations; and finally the beauty and grace of the Radiguet warships are unparalleled in finesse, and as curator I have had the pleasure of firing up their splendid steam plants.

Q. Can you identify a few boats that have an unusually high number of functional features, such as cannons that fire?

A. The *Kasuga* has a timing mechanism that, when wound up, runs the ship out a bit, fires a gun, then turns it 90 degrees and another 90 degrees to head back. The large Märklin warships were filled with cannons that, with a small powder charge, would fire when the fuse was lit. On battery-operated boats of big size, lights could be illuminated as well. The large warship from the Paris toy shop Nain-Jaune had a gas-fired steam plant that is huge, and though I have never fired it up, I'm sure in its day it was truly the ultimate toy. Some of the floor toys, when pulled, had an off-center set of wheels, so that when dragged along they bobbed up and down in a wave-like motion. Probably the most dramatic special effect occurred in the submarines, which, when wound up, ran along the surface, then dove for a few feet, and then resurfaced, all great fun so long as the sub didn't get stuck in the mud on a pond's bottom!

Q. Of the toys in the collection, are there any you're personally particularly proud of acquiring, finding, or selecting?

A. While there are many stories to be told of acquiring the various pieces, the most fun ones were where the hunt led finally to an acquisition of a real gem. As with the large battleship, *Posen*, I received a letter and a photo from someone who had heard we had paid a large sum for a toy boat; and would I be interested in theirs? It had been in the family for many decades, but it was time to sell. It took a while to locate them in upstate New York, but when I did, they told me of the boat's origins: their grandfather had been a soldier in Europe during the First War and had bought it and had shipped it home. Sadly he was killed shortly after, and this was kept, in the shipping crate, as a memory of him. Other times the chase led to disappointment, starting with what looked great in a photo or described in a letter, but then turned out to be either an outright fake or a once fine toy now terribly repainted or badly restored. I did make a trip to France once to chase down a group of boats being offered in an obscure local sale; they were quite surprised to find a Yank in their midst buying all the boats.

Q. Are you pretty much finished with acquisitions, or is there something that you don't have that you would like to see in the collection?

A. No collection is ever really finished, so there are examples I would still like to have, but when my father died, I stopped adding to it; it had been something we had done together, and I felt satisfied that we had done a fine job. The display at the Forbes Galleries is a testament to the fun we had, so I have left it that way.

Q. What can you tell us about people outside the Forbes family who helped make the collection what it is?

A. In the early days, there were a few individuals who were very kind to us and steered us in the direction of some of our best finds. There was Tom Sage in Pennsylvania, a train collector who had a bunch of boats that he was willing to part with, not just because he was a toy dealer, but because he saw our enthusiasm. He and his family gladly shared their helpful knowledge. Certainly one of the deans of the business is David Pressland, whose magnificent book, *The Art of the Tin Toy,* was a huge inspiration for us. David was always kind and never hesitated to help when he could. My mentor in this strange world of antique toys was Jacques Millet, with whom I co-authored the book, *Toy Boats 1870–1955: A Pictorial History.* Jacques, who passed away this year, was an expert's expert who loved the world he was involved in and summed it all up by saying that, for him, "These toys are like a caress from childhood."

Q. Your father once said that you amassed greater knowledge of rare toy boats than he possessed. Are there specific areas where you feel your knowledge is particularly keen?

A. As I helped put together the collection, my knowledge grew; it had to. We were receiving many replies to our ads in trade publications like *Antique Toy World*, and I had to be able to understand what they were trying to peddle. Because various manufacturers had merged over the years, I needed to know what were distinguishing features for correct identification. So I started to put together as comprehensive a toy library as I could, gathering reproductions and originals of manufacturer's catalogues, sales brochures, and the like. Because we were after examples from all makers, of all sizes, I needed all the information I could find. Besides, it was plain fun for this bathtub admiral to be well versed in the area toward which we were putting a fair amount of resources.

Q. Has your passion for this collection diminished over the years? Today, emotionally, how much does it mean to you? Is it a kind of link to your father and grandfather? Does it still conjure up memories of your youth?

A. I have not invested much time in the collection since my father's passing. It was something we did together, and indeed, it is a precious link we had. Of all my siblings, I enjoyed boats the most, whether making models from kits or out of materials at hand, so the collection was a way to relive some of that pleasure. Every time I wander through the Galleries, I feel the connection to these pieces and the fun we had assembling them. I still like to mess around in boats, and nowadays get supreme pleasure from rowing my wife around a New Hampshire lake in the summertime in a lovely old rowboat called the *Daiseybelle*, a Thames skiff from the '30s that I bought in England, whose lovely lines remind me of just how pretty a boat on the water can be.

CARETTE STEAM ENGINE

BIBLIOGRAPHY

"Capitalist Toys: A Selection of Toy Boats and Toy Motorcycles from
The Forbes Magazine Collection," a booklet published for the Sotheby's auction, December 19, 1994.

Forbes, Malcolm, "My Fantasy Fleet," *Art & Antiques*, July 19, 1989, 2–5.

Forbes, Robert and Jacques Milet. *Toy Boats 1870–1955: A Pictorial History*.
New York: Charles Scribner's Sons, 1979.

Pressland, David. *The Art of the Tin Toy*. New York: Crown Publishers, Inc., 1976.

Remise, Jac and Jean Fondin. *The Golden Age of Toys*. Lausanne, Switzerland: Edita S.A., 1967.

About the Author

Richard Scholl has been a consultant, an award-winning creative director, and an author who has written about collectibles and the industry for decades. He is the author of *Matchbox Official 50th Anniversary Edition* (2002), a comprehensive pictorial history book that won rave reviews internationally. Scholl has written numerous articles on collecting and was managing editor of *The Matchbox Collector*, a newsletter published by Matchbox Collectibles for many years. Scholl worked at the Franklin Mint for several years and has since developed advertising and reference material for many of America's most prominent direct marketers of collectibles, including the Hamilton Collection, Lenox, Bradford Exchange, Action Performance, Ashton-Drake Galleries, Corgi Classics, Disney, and America Remembers. Scholl has also worked for toy companies including Tyco Preschool and Tyco R/C. A published poet, Scholl is the author of *The Running Press Glossary of Baseball Language* and has been a research consultant and contributor to many other books published by Running Press. An adjunct professor of communications at Drexel University in Philadelphia for nineteen years and, more recently, professor at West Chester University in West Chester, Pa., Scholl is president of the Scholl Group, a full-service advertising, communications, and marketing firm. He earned his bachelor of arts degree in writing and his master's degree in English from The Pennsylvania State University. Born in Pittsburgh, Richard now resides in Bryn Mawr, Pennsylvania, with his wife, Catherine, and their two children, Geoffrey and Jennifer. Scholl has also recently written another book celebrating the world's most comprehensive collection of toy soldiers, housed in the same place where the world's most comprehensive collection of toy boats is on display—the Forbes Galleries in New York City.